The Symphony of Your Life

Restoring Harmony When Your World Is Out of Tune

MARK HARDCASTLE

Copyright © 2014, 2017, 2019 by Mark Hardcastle. All rights reserved.

No part of this publication may be reproduced, stored in a retrieval system, or transmitted in any form or by any means, electrical, mechanical, photocopying, recording, scanning, or otherwise, except as permitted under the most current United States Copyright Statute, without the prior written permission of the copyright holder. Requests for permission should be addressed to the Permissions Department, Symphony Books LLC, 5994 S. Holly Street #112, Greenwood Village, CO 80111. Requests may also be emailed to info@symphonyofyourlife.com.

Published by Symphony Books LLC, 5994 S. Holly Street #112, Greenwood Village, CO 80111
Website: www.SymphonyOfYourLife.com. Contact: info@symphonyofyourlife.com

Editor: Jennifer Thomas
Jacket Design: Lisa Conner
Body Design: Jennifer Thomas

Limit of Liability/Disclaimer of Warranty: While the publisher and author have used their best efforts in preparing this book, they make no representations or warranties with respect to the accuracy or completeness of the contents of this book and specifically disclaim any implied warranties of merchantability or fitness for a particular purpose. No warranty may be created or extended by sales representatives or written sales materials. This book is intended for motivation and inspiration only and should not be relied upon for any other purpose. The advice and strategies contained herein may not be suitable for your situation. You should consult with a professional where appropriate. Neither the publisher nor author shall be liable for any loss of profit or any other commercial damages, including but not limited to special, incidental, consequential, or any other damages of any kind. Where referral is made to actual persons, names may have been changed to protect privacy.

Permissions:

p. 3: "Sure on this Shining Night" from PERMIT ME VOYAGE by James Agee. Copyright © 1968 by the James Agee Trust, used by permission of The Wylie Agency LLC.

p. 43: "Someone To Watch Over Me" (from "Oh, Kay"). Music and Lyrics by GEORGE GERSHWIN and IRA GERSHWIN © 1926 (Renewed) WB MUSIC CORP. All rights reserved. Used by Permission of ALFRED MUSIC PUBLISHING CO., INC.

p. 76: Quote from CHANCY by Louis L'Amour, copyright © 1976 by Louis L'Amour. Copyright renewed (c) 1996 by Katherine L'Amour, Beau L'Amour, and Angelique L'Amour. Used by permission of Bantam Books, a division of Random House, Inc. Any third party use of this material, outside of this publication, is prohibited. Interested parties must apply directly to Random House, Inc. for permission.

Publisher's Cataloging-in-Publication
(Provided by Quality Books, Inc.)

Hardcastle, Mark, 1959-
   The symphony of your life : restoring harmony when your world is out of tune / by Mark Hardcastle.
   p. cm.
   LCCN 2013935817
   ISBN 978-0-9857057-1-8

   1. Success--Psychological aspects.   I. Title.
BF637.S8H37 2013   158.1
                           QBI13-600054

ISBN: 978-0-9600821-0-0 Paperback
First Edition

To Luke, Anna, Seth, and Cameron

I hope this book helps you build lives fully formed:
unique selves governed by fierce integrity.
You've started well.
I'm proud of each one of you!

Contents

Foreword: You Can—You Really, Really Can!   viii

Preface: Is Anyone Conducting the Concert?   xiv

Acknowledgments   xxviii

Introduction: The Wheel of Fortune   4
    Have You Been in the Circle
    with Yin and Yang Lately?   8
    Where Are You on *Your* Wheel?   12

Chapter 1   Surviving the Dark Ages   18
    What Is *Your* Story So Far?   27

Chapter 2   It Isn't Always About You   32
    What's Your Response?   42

Contents

Chapter 3	The Power of One	52
	Whose Wheels Have Turned with Yours?	59
Chapter 4	Be the Spark	64
	Whose Wheel Can You Kick-Start?	74
Chapter 5	Seek Out Greatness	80
	What Is Your Passion?	86
Chapter 6	Live *Your* Best Life	92
	Whose Life Are You Living?	97
Chapter 7	If You're Still Breathing, It Wasn't Fatal	102
	Do You Jump?	110
	What Have You Learned?	116
Chapter 8	Prepare. Respond. Keep Running.	122
	Are You Still Running?	133
Chapter 9	It's Better to Be Right Than Wise	140
	What Would You Do Over?	147
Chapter 10	Creating Your Symphony	154
Afterword: Where Are They Now?		166
About the Author		175

Foreword

You Can—
You Really, Really Can!

"I THINK I SHOULD write your Foreword."

"I appreciate the thought, but don't you think there might be a credibility issue?"

"Proving your methods on your wife must count for something!"

In short, I was the guinea pig for this book.

As Mark was fleshing out and documenting his ideas, I found myself face-to-face with a series of challenges: I watched our mutual employer go bankrupt. After we married, I moved over four thousand miles from my home in England to start a new life in the U.S. I fought numerous self-improvement battles and headed down a brand new career path.

Foreword: You Can—You Really, Really Can!

All the while, Mark gave me courage to continue forward by reminding me of the quintessential concepts, catchphrases, and methodologies he was developing to convey his philosophies. These simple yet powerful formulas are extremely valuable life lessons boiled down into easy-to-remember "mini-mantras," which proved to be lifesavers when I was trying to recover from a setback or was unsure how to proceed.

They *really* worked!

Thanks to Mark's inspiration-injections, I effectively restored harmony to my life. I am now a successful business owner, which is an accomplishment I'm extremely proud of!

Starting my own business was scary. My idea was as pie in the sky as it could get—at least that's how I perceived it. But Mark doesn't think like that, fortunately for me—*and* for you, dear reader!

I had a vision of what I wanted, but should I really go for it? Following Mark's advice, his call for solid analysis, and his encouragement to live *my* best life…yes, I "jumped"!

One of my favorite mantras is presented in *Chapter 8: Prepare. Respond. Keep Running.* That's exactly what it took to get my business off the ground.

I started off with a half-rental in an antique mall, reselling "vintage" items for next to no profit. *Respond!* I generated a little more profit by painting old bits of furniture and reselling them; but it was still sporadic and not enough. *Respond again! Keep running!*

The Symphony of Your Life / Mark Hardcastle

I was struck by an idea: *Ahaaaaa! Kitchen cabinets! Yes, people are sick of the sea of oak! What can I do? I can paint! And if I can paint, then I can paint kitchen cabinets.* But, but, but—

Which leads me to another of Mark's teachings: "You can. You just need to know you can!"

Yes, I can. Now, dozens of kitchens later, with money in the bank, I know I can!

But there were more setbacks—there always are. "Sometimes you're the windshield and sometimes you're the bug," Mark likes to say. You *are* going to fall on your nose, maybe more than once. Mark helped me internalize that even though today you may be the poor little bug, tomorrow you will be the windshield. But only if you believe it and keep running.

Case in point: My business was going beautifully. I had partnered with another painter, who was organized and had a marvelous corporate background. And while our methods differed, we balanced that out with our talents. Until, one day, the windshield bore down on me, and… *Splat!* My partner announced that she wanted to go it alone. Definitely a "bug" experience!

But sure enough, it wasn't long before *I* became the windshield. I discovered that I'm perfectly able to function as a sole proprietor, without the corporate knowledge that I thought I so desperately needed. Turns out, I don't! And now *I* get to call all the shots.

I prepared, I responded, and I kept running. In doing so, I got further than I had ever dreamed!

And while I may have a bias towards my husband's work, I've also had the unique opportunity to follow the stories in the book as they unfolded, attend Mark's many workshops, video record his speaking gigs, and listen to him rehearse. I've even been lucky enough to receive a goodly amount of coaching across the breakfast table.

The result?

I can firmly attest that the techniques and lesson-packed stories highlighted within—though each can stand alone—together provide a magnificent foundation on which to build *your* best life.

So read on, assimilate, and remember—seriously: *You can. You really, really can!* Take it from me!

Judi Hockenhull
CEO, Girls Who Paint, LLC
Centennial, Colorado
www.girlswhopaint.com
facebook.com/girlswhopaint

"Writing a book is an adventure.
To begin with, it is a toy and an amusement;
then it becomes a mistress, and then it becomes a master,
and then a tyrant.
The last phase is that just as you are about to be reconciled
to your servitude, you kill the monster and
fling him out to the public."

—Sir Winston Churchill

Preface

Is Anyone Conducting the Concert?

I SUPPOSE ANY AUTHOR is fascinated by every book he writes. He wouldn't sit down to write unless he thought he had something to say. But having just completed this journey, I wonder whether other authors' books take on lives of their own and end up saying things quite different from the author's original ideas. That was certainly my experience.

Early on, I enjoyed watching the ideas evolve as they casually appeared line by line on my laptop over weeks, then months, of writing. Before I knew it, my "toy" was a couple of years old, and there was no real push to get it finished within any particular timeframe.

Then I broke my neck.

Preface: Is Anyone Conducting the Concert?

Of course, I didn't know I was on the way to breaking my neck; I was merely out for a mountain bike adventure with my pals. However, I am pretty sure I wasn't focused enough on the trail that day.

I became very focused, though, when I found myself flat on my back looking up at the blue sky, with somebody shouting at me not to move. The voice belonged to another cyclist who had ridden up just as I was regaining consciousness. Clarity rode up with him.

It is not possible to overstate the potential severity of my accident. I was launched headfirst into the rocky terrain, splintering five vertebrae in my neck. It was bad.

But it could have been worse. Had I not impacted the ground like a spear, with no twisting or bending, the force of the crash would surely have snapped my spinal cord. It would have been all over for me.

So, for someone who broke his neck in multiple places, I got off easy. Several months of healing have made it possible for me to return to my previous life (sans bicycles, at least for now). Normalcy is trying to return.

But after you've broken your neck, what is normal?

Having come so close to lights out, I assure you that, yes, I am now focused. "Normal" has become a heightened sense of urgency to get certain things done.

Writing this book is one of those things. In the time it took me to fly over the handlebars and break my neck (along with a handful of ribs!), this "adventure" stopped being an "amusement," swept through "mistress" and "master," and became a "tyrant."

Now the monster has been slain. The book is in your hands. So let me tell you why I wrote it to begin with.

THIS PROJECT GOT ITS START as the Great Recession of 2008 became full-throated. Real estate values were free-falling in earnest, and my employer, a major international airline that had recently emerged from a near-fatal bankruptcy, was whispering about doing it all over again in the face of record oil prices and declining demand for air travel. Facing potential unemployment, I found myself reflecting on the ups and downs of my life, and a key realization surfaced: *No matter how bad things looked at any particular point, they always seemed to get better with time.*

Good things happen in bad times.

What a simple concept. But one we often overlook.

It's a fact of life that bad things happen. We know this. What we sometimes fail to acknowledge is that good things inevitably happen as well. Mark Hardcastle is nobody special in that regard.

When I entered my fifties, I saw that the trend was consistent enough to contain a germ of faith. Could I *rely*

Preface: Is Anyone Conducting the Concert?

on the idea that Fortune is not so scornful as to bring only adversity? Apparently so, if the pattern of my life was to be believed.

While my airline colleagues and I spoke about our careers and our prospects going into the future, I began writing about my past experiences as a way of staying optimistic. From time to time, I'd show my musings to other pilots, and the stories often resonated.

My thoughts formed themselves into chapters, and next thing I knew, I had a book in the making. But what did I want it to accomplish?

In its infancy, my book contained only stories illustrating how good things often follow life's challenges. That was nice enough.

Then a colleague pointed out that stories alone might not encourage folks to apply my ideas to their own lives. He suggested I find a way to involve my readers in the stories—ask them to find their own meaning as they read.

And that's when I knew this could be an anthology of hope. If my stories could lead others to their own solutions, then this project would have real value for real lives in a moment of historic hardship.

But something was still missing. Is life really all about chance? Or can we somehow influence our fate? If so, does that mean we pretty much bring our own sufferings down upon ourselves? More importantly, can we do anything to self-correct when we find ourselves off course?

Sure, bad things happen to good people. And good things often follow. But how can we influence the process to make sure those good things ultimately come our way?

When I was a senior cadet at the United States Air Force (USAF) Academy, I took a class to study the writings of Shakespeare. On the final exam, the professor posed this question:

> *In Lesson 1, your instructor said he wanted you to be happier in December than you were in August. What could he possibly have meant by that?*

My response was this:

> *As a result of this course, we should have a bit more knowledge of the world and its ways. Whether or not the knowledge itself is comforting, we should derive some comfort in having it. The game is always more fun if you know how to play it well.*

Some of that knowledge has to do with the real risk that we as individuals have tragic flaws that lead us into trouble. We would do well to become aware of those potential trouble spots. I think of a fellow I once knew whose self-awareness had reached a level that kept him from even walking onto a used car lot because he knew he couldn't say no. Good for him!

Preface: Is Anyone Conducting the Concert?

More of that knowledge is the understanding that those we interact with often have their own motivations that could do us harm—intentionally or not. That used car salesman who's just trying to make a living, for example, would be eager to sell my buddy a car, even if it wasn't in my friend's best interest.

And so, when we are overwhelmed by circumstances like personal bankruptcy or home foreclosure, it can be hard for us to feel certain that there is good in the world and hope for our future. But we *do* know that, right?

Okay, so how do we know?

We can use life's patterns.

Even in the darkest of hours, we are surrounded by templates—patterns in our own life stories to which we can turn for guidance. Sometimes we see them; sometimes we don't.

These templates are part of why we study the works of Shakespeare. Through his plays and poetry, Shakespeare has illustrated for us his observations about how the world works. We apply that information by figuring out how to minimize the frequency with which we find ourselves in harm's way. Perhaps more importantly: when we do get into trouble (as we inevitably will), his templates help us find our way back to safety and prosperity.

This book provides a few templates from my life. They're stories of how I've responded to life events. How I've tried to influence the process so those good things would indeed come my way—sometimes successfully, sometimes less so—and how I've seen those lessons from Shakespeare put to work around me. My stories are filled with villains and heroes, good characters and bad, all from the real world. They tell of some situations that didn't end well and the tools I used to recover.

My hope is to pass these tools on to you. More importantly, I hope my stories springboard you to your own past, to remind you of how *you've* persevered before.

The bottom line: We've all been down. We've all recovered. Why should this time, or next time, be any different? We can and should use the resources we've used in the past, as well as new resources, to handle the next rough patch. We absolutely *can* influence our life process and make sure those good things come our way!

When we're on top of Fortune's "Wheel" (more on that later!) and times are good, let's enjoy them while they're here. We can know that even when the good times pass, we'll have the resources to get ourselves to the top again.

Preface: Is Anyone Conducting the Concert?

As this manuscript morphed into its final form, I met with my friend and accomplished author Mark Hoog, CEO of Growing Field International, Inc., to get his opinion of how to get this particular tool into as many hands as possible. He suggested I use my involvement in the world of choral music as a metaphor to unify the various illustrations in this book. Indeed, my being a conductor is central to my stories.

That's when the Symphony of Your Life series was born.

The goal of this series is to help you decide what you want the "concert" of your own life to look like. And to inspire you to organize your own metaphorical Symphony—to recruit your own musicians, gather the music you want to play, rent out the concert hall, and perform the concert *you* want to perform.

Conductor's Notes

When you've attended actual concerts, as opposed to metaphorical ones, you may have noticed Conductor's Notes in the printed program. These are intended to help you understand what you are hearing. I've used the same idea here to guide you through each chapter. They'll look like this!

Preface: Is Anyone Conducting the Concert?

As we went to print for the first edition of this book in 2014, the seismic event that inspired the project, the Great Recession of 2008, was abating. The optimism of the next "up" cycle was beginning to manifest.

Now, as we go to print for the second time three years later, I want to let you know how the project has been received.

When my mentor, Mark Hoog, speaks at elementary schools, he tells a fun story about the evolution of the cell phone. (While one might argue the virtue of elementary students having cell phones, the fact that they do is undeniable. And it allows for a teachable moment.)

Mark first explains that when he was their age, phones were attached to the wall by cables. When he was a bit older, someone thought up the idea of cordless phones and, next thing you knew, folks could walk around the house while talking, as long as they were within range of the base station. In due course, somebody imagined a phone that didn't need a base station, and cell phones were born. The world will never be the same!

Mark's point, of course, is that it all started with a dream.

Mark closes by asking the kids: "Who has a big dream—a dream that will change the world? A dream so big you can't wait to make it happen?" He then urges them to: "Hurry up! You're going to change our world! We're waiting on you! Hurry up!"

I thought of that story in early April of 2014 when I received my two proof copies of the book from the printer.

It was my neighborhood's annual garage sale, so as neighbors do, I set up my lawn chair at the top of the driveway and littered my yard with stuff I no longer needed. Then I pulled out one of my two copies. For the next hour or so, I reveled in having completed the project after so many years and in how it had turned out. By now you've seen the beautiful artwork Lisa Conner created for the dust jacket, and Jennifer Thomas's masterful interior layout and graphics, so you can appreciate how I felt just looking at it. Euphoric would not be too strong a word.

Just after lunchtime, a minivan rolled up. As a group of adults spilled onto my sidewalk, a lady called out: "That must be a great book, from the look on your face!"

In an embarrassingly childish way, I jumped out of my chair, ran up, and handed her the book. I was like a puppy seeking approval.

She ran her fingers over the violin on the front as everybody does, then she turned the book over and read the back cover. She took her time reading the flaps and flipping through the pages. Finally she looked up.

"I think this book might help me," she said.

My heart leapt, but I managed to control myself as I inquired why she said that. She lifted the hem of her sweatshirt to reveal a pouch of liquid with a line into her abdomen. It was chemotherapy medicine. "I'm fighting breast cancer," she explained.

Without hesitation, I grabbed a pen and inscribed the book to her. There was no selflessness in the gesture; it was

Preface: Is Anyone Conducting the Concert?

something I was simply driven to do. I thought of Mark's challenge to the kids: "Hurry up! We're waiting on you!" And I could sense the Universe saying, "Thank you, Mark. We've been waiting on you. We'll take it from here."

A few months later, I received an email from the woman's neighbor, expressing how much the stories had meant to her dear friend.

And the Universe has indeed "taken it from here."

Right after the book came out, my friend Brian, who is a captain for my airline, graciously purchased a copy. Brian has a brother who also flies for our airline, as did their father before them. Brian's son, David, has grown up to be a pilot as well, and would of course like to join the family legacy of flying for our airline. So, a few months ago he went through the application process.

And was turned down.

Right about then, he found his dad's copy of my book on the coffee table and started to read. I soon received a note from Brian telling me his son had found encouragement in its message.

Then this arrived from David himself:

> *I was blessed with* The Symphony of Your Life *at a time when I needed it most. Having suffered a major setback in my career that wasn't easy for me or my family, your book gave me greater perspective on the bigger picture. I found comfort not just in reading about your personal*

struggles, but through the reassurance that all will work out for the better given time and persistence.

My favorite line from the book, which has played over and over in my mind, is from Chapter 1: "Sometimes the good stuff coming down the road doesn't show up for a while."

I am now able to stay in the process and move forward with anticipation of what the Universe has in store for me.

I am so gratified by David's feedback. It confirms that *my* job remains to get the message out there—which is what this second printing is all about. My book can continue to find its way to those who need it, as it did to the woman with cancer, to David, and to so many others who have taken the time to write to me.

And now, it's found its way to you.

Since this book is in your hands, I trust that you, too, will find inspiration and encouragement in its message. Thank you for picking it up!

—Mark

Acknowledgments

THIS BOOK IS A COLLABORATION. Not in the sense that several people sat together in a room to create it. Rather, I've had the joy of sharing my ideas with lots of individuals who provided their own feedback, which ultimately became a part of my message.

I fear I have neglected to keep as complete a list as I should have of those who've helped me along the way. To those I have omitted, please forgive me. I appreciated your insights! Those I have managed to recollect are named below with my thanks. I am in your debt!

I cannot thank my friend and mentor Mark Hoog enough. He is the one who first suggested that I might have a story to tell and then encouraged

Acknowledgments

me to tell it. He has already accomplished in his own life what I hope to achieve with this book. If I have succeeded, it's because I have followed his lead as closely as I could.

Next there's fellow pilot Steve Lerum, who waded through one of the earliest, roughest drafts and rendered the opinion that, indeed, there may be a book hidden within what was still twaddle at the time.

Dr. Z. Randall Stroope years ago saw a musical potential in me that I wasn't sure was there and encouraged me to feed and water it and see what grew. In fact, he walked beside me and did a fair amount of the cultivation himself.

My colleague from the Colorado Children's Chorale, Anne Stylianou, a wordsmith in her own right and the truest bibliophile I know, gave me her time and extraordinary focus when both of those were needed for more important work in her own life, as did fellow authors and thought leaders Rachel Schultz and Lisa Ford.

Coach Al Abeyta was my son's football coach. During the three seasons I talk about in Chapter 9, he was the quintessential teacher. He taught the sport well. He taught life lessons better. My son is the person he is because of things he learned from Coach Abeyta.

Debbie DeSantis from the Colorado Children's Chorale, fellow pilots Dave Gottschalk and Joe Yanacek, and speaker/author Mark Sanborn all provided important encouragement and constructive feedback along the way.

Real estate mentors Gary Keller, Jim Slinkard, and Larry Girard inspired, encouraged, and taught me how to be a successful real estate agent. More importantly, they reinforced in me the ideas that I've tried to pass on in this book.

My thanks go out to each of these folks for the roles they've played in helping me understand the world as I do. Without any one of them, this book might not have happened. Without all of them, it would not be what it is.

I also can't say enough about my creative team!

Lisa Conner of Zeto Creative possessed the magic required to produce the dust jacket, which I knew was exceptional the moment I saw it. I can now report that it's not unusual for a reader's hand to go straight to the violin—a visceral response that is no longer surprising but still gratifying!

Acknowledgments

And then there's my editor, Jennifer Thomas of Beyond Words Editing, who masterfully kept me from going off the rails at a number of critical points. Her content editing skills combined with technical expertise made sure I was saying what I was trying to say. In addition, her talent at page layout and design gave you the gorgeous interior graphics you're about to enjoy. Thanks, Jennifer!

Finally, I would be beyond remiss if I did not acknowledge the constant encouragement from my wife, Judi, and my four kids, Luke, Anna, Seth, and Cameron. They have all been as eager to see this book in its final form as I have, and have put up with my disappearances when I was off working on the manuscript. Thank you. Your support made this project possible.

Introduction

The Wheel of Fortune

THERE'S A SYMBOL common to Far Eastern cultures of two tadpole-like creatures confined within a circle, swimming eternally toward each other. One is completely black, save for its white eye. Its twin is white with a black eye.

In many ways these creatures, Yin and Yang, are identical. They are the same size and shape. They each have one eye. And each has precisely the same lot in life as the other, the pair locked together for eternity within the confines of their single circular universe.

Simultaneously, however, they are opposites: a white eye on a black body versus a black eye on a white body; one facing up and left, the other down and right.

What are we to glean from this dichotomy of unity and difference? Simply, that the dichotomy exists. Yin and Yang

Introduction: The Wheel of Fortune

are constant advocates for the duality of our existence. We live in a dual world: male and female, good and evil, light and dark. We speak of the pros and cons of a decision, rich versus poor, bright and dim, hot and cold.

These Yin-Yang blacks and whites are the poles that help us clarify our lives. Rarely, however, are things quite so absolute. Clarity is often obscured by the myriad shades of gray within which we find ourselves. Yet by definition, always within the gray are both the black and the white. And we often have the power to choose which predominates.

ANOTHER LESSON WE CAN GLEAN from Yin and Yang has to do with the circle that confines them.

In 1935, American composer Carl Orff published a work he entitled "Carmina Burana." The text was taken from a series of writings found in a monastery near Munich, Germany, apparently penned by medieval monks.

The theme of the work, naturally, is described in the opening movement. The first line reads: "O, Fortuna, velut luna, statu variabilis," referring to Fortune, which like the moon, comes and goes. The song goes on to enumerate circumstances one might encounter during a lifetime in which life is sometimes good and sometimes hard—in other words, a normal life. The entire work expands upon that theme. Sometimes you're up; sometimes you're down. (Or as we used to say in the rural South where I grew up, sometimes you're the windshield; sometimes you're the bug!)

The Symphony of Your Life / Mark Hardcastle

On the cover of the sheet music is a drawing of a wheel: the Wheel of Fortune.

In this medieval rendering of the ancient legend, Fortune is represented by a goddess who sits in the center of her Wheel and controls its seemingly capricious turns. Out on the edge are four characters whose positions represent their current lots in life. On the left side of the wheel is the ambitious prince who is about to reign. At the top is the fortunate king who is reigning. Opposite the prince is the deposed king whose reign has ended. And at the bottom of the wheel sits the poor soul without a kingdom.

This singular image of the Wheel of Fortune contains the whole of "Carmina Burana." Indeed, it contains the story of life itself.

The image is completed by this rather ominous inscription:

> *The wheel of Fortune turns;*
> *I go down, demeaned;*
> *another is carried to the height.*

The cycle of human existence described symbolically by the medieval Wheel of Fortune is real. We've all experienced the pessimism and sense of helplessness it expresses.

But it *is* a wheel—a circle, rather than a straight line. What are we to make of that?

Yin and Yang remind us that what goes around comes around; the Wheel of Fortune turns. We see an elegant

Introduction: The Wheel of Fortune

circle of life all around us. Organisms live, die, decay, and provide sustenance for the new life that rises from the dust. Summer gives way to fall, but winter always gives way to spring, which must then become summer again. The sun passes from east to west each and every day; each and every night, it passes from west to east again while we sleep. Bad things happen to good people. And, of course, good things happen to bad people.

Have You Been in the Circle with Yin and Yang Lately?

How did The Great Recession of 2008 manifest in your life? Was it, for you, much ado about nothing? Did you own your home free and clear? Did you remain untouched by the foreclosure scandals that followed the Wall Street meltdown? Were you retired with your savings mostly in cash and unaffected by the fall in stocks?

On the other hand, were you, like many, less fortunate? When the economy tanks, jobs are lost. When companies go bankrupt, pensions are lost. When stocks fall, savings are lost. Did any of that apply to you?

What, then, did you do?

Introduction: The Wheel of Fortune

HAVE YOU EVER BEEN for a ride on an old-fashioned carousel? You know, those massive old merry-go-rounds where you sit on the horses that go up and down while the organ music plays?

In years gone by, carousel operators enticed folks onto the ride by giving them a chance to win a second ride for free. All the rider had to do was grab the brass ring that was positioned just out of reach as they went around the circle.

Of course, if you missed the ring the first time you went by, you could always try again on the next pass, or the next.

Over time, the idea of "grabbing the brass ring" became a metaphor for life in general. To say you'd caught the brass ring meant you'd achieved your goals or realized your ambitions.

Part of the lesson from Yin and Yang is that Fortune is capricious indeed. She lifts us toward our ambitions—our brass rings that wait at the top of her Grand Wheel—only to scuttle us away again.

But if the Wheel of Fortune is not the whole story, what else should we be looking for?

The part that the Wheel inscription leaves out is that we need not be mere passengers, like the poor princes out on the margins. We have a say. We can put on the brakes if needed, or we can give the Wheel a push of our own. We need only recognize where we are on the Wheel at any given time, and then figure out how to deal with that reality.

Have you just missed your brass ring? How can you keep the Wheel moving? Are you getting close? How do you slow it down?

And what do you do if the Wheel seems to stop altogether before you get to the ring?

Quite simply, you stay in the process.

JAMES AGEE'S POEM "Sure on This Shining Night," to me, speaks about living after terrible loss, reminding us that life goes on.

Dark times of loss and pain will occur; it's part of the human condition. But so is our capacity for healing. We can recover over time. And in fact we should. We need not deny the grieving that is so much a part of healthy recovery. Nor, though, need we grieve forever.

Agee's poem, while beautiful and replete with meaning, is not unique. Popular culture as well as classical literature is filled with the musings of poets who have understood the same thing; thoughts that have improved our ability to survive periods of darkness and then go on, often more able than before. Even today's pop music is infused with Nietzsche's famous line "That which does not kill us makes us stronger."

These ideas continue to appear in modern culture and I imagine they always will. Why? Because they encourage. They encourage because they are true.

Better times are ahead.

Loss is not the only way we experience darkness. It is also part of the human condition that we progress through life in fits and starts. We stumble, catch ourselves, and move on. We fall again, pick ourselves up again, and yes, move on again. We enjoy. We endure. We struggle. We thrive. Bad things happen, good things happen—sometimes very bad, sometimes very good.

The final word for us from Yin and Yang is that as long as they keep swimming toward each other, we will have another chance at the rings. Better times are always just around the next turn.

Where Are You on *Your* Wheel?

There is a world in which we live. It may not be the world in which we'd like to live. Yin and Yang had no say about which circle they ended up in. People, places, events, and things that we have no control over will, from time to time, impact us. Once we accept that reality, we can accurately assess where we are and decide how best to move forward. The arc of our lives has less to do with Fortune herself than with how we respond to her.

Today, are you the windshield or are you the bug? Have you grasped your brass rings? Or do you need to go around again? Are you starting to realize that maybe you have yet to define your rings?

Ask yourself: In a perfect world, one in which you are reigning at the top of your Wheel, what will you be doing with your life?

What is the best way to get there from where you are now?

What do you need to do to turn your Wheel?

Introduction: The Wheel of Fortune

Conductor's Notes

What do you want your orchestra to look like? Do you aspire to conduct a great philharmonic? Or will you enjoy the intimacy of a small band? What does it look like right now?

Some great orchestras in large metropolitan areas seem to prosper regardless of the state of the world. It was not always that way. They achieved their status by growing through times of adversity and by their thoughtful responses to "bad" fortune. Expect ups and downs on your way to realizing your vision for your orchestra.

Don't lose sight of the duality of our world. There is light and dark, good and bad; each hardship we survive enables us to better handle the next one. Regardless of how your orchestra looks today, you can change it with any turn of the Wheel.

WE'VE LOOKED AT SOME QUESTIONS in this Introduction. Answering these questions and more is what this book is about.

Fortune spins her Wheel. But that doesn't mean we're helpless—just along for the ride. We can impact how often and how fast the Wheel turns. We have a say in how quickly we go from being "without a kingdom" to "about to reign."

My hope is that the stories in this book will stimulate your creative thinking. I encourage you to consider how you might apply these ideas to your life as it is today in order to get your Wheel moving again in the right direction. In fact, I encourage you to keep a pen and paper handy to make notes as you read. And I hope these ideas will help you rebuild your resources so you'll be ready for whatever Fortune throws your way in days to come!

"Nothing in this world can take the place of persistence. Talent will not; nothing is more common than unsuccessful people with talent. Genius will not; unrewarded genius is almost a proverb. Education will not; the world is full of educated derelicts. Persistence and determination alone are omnipotent. The slogan 'press on' has solved and always will solve the problems of the human race."

—Calvin Coolidge

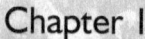

Chapter 1

Surviving the Dark Ages

WHEN I WAS IN HIGH SCHOOL, I was a brash lad. In the "wisdom" of my youth, I was fully aware that nothing was impossible. No thing could not be achieved. Everything I could see or imagine was within my grasp. The quote beside my portrait in my high school yearbook was what I lived by:

> *"A man's reach should exceed his grasp,*
> *else what's a heaven for?"*
>
> —Robert Browning

With that as a foundation, one would think a young student would have a plan, a specific ambition. Not me. I had no idea where I would go in life. Many wise people had suggested that I follow my dreams. Do what I loved. That if

I could find an occupation that paid me to do what I love, I'd never work a day in my life.

For me, that would have involved music in some way. But I also knew that being a musician was a hard way to make a living. Many of those same mentors who advised me to pursue my passions were quick to remind me that some passions pay better than others! So I chose to convert my love of music to an avocation while trying to find another way to earn my keep. One day, maybe, after I'd made my fortune, I could come back to music and have my choir or orchestra. The seed would stay in the ground for now, and time would tell.

As an alternative to music, I knew that airline piloting held great promise. But because I had relatively poor eyesight, I had no realistic expectation of a flying career. The Air Force could provide the requisite schooling and experience, but they required perfect vision for pilots. And while some civilians could afford their own training, I wasn't one of them. So it looked like such a livelihood wasn't in the cards.

But what about the non-flying armed forces? I had always thought that the military in general was cool. I loved the way my dad reminisced about the tragic heroics of the great World War II in which he'd fought. And I was a sucker for all those John Wayne movies, unrealistic as they ultimately were. So with no further direction, I headed off toward the United States Air Force Academy, anticipating a good job out of college and maybe a sense of direction before my hitch was through.

On that grand Wheel, one could have said I was on top. I certainly would have said as much. However, as Fortune would have it, a precipitous pitch-over loomed in my near future. I didn't see it coming.

MY FIRST INDICATION that things were not what I'd expected arrived on my very first morning in the cadet dormitory. As my roommates and I were settling into our new living spaces the afternoon before, the upperclassmen had taken many of our effects and placed them safely into storage for us. As part of that process, they had taken our watches, clocks, and anything else that might help us keep track of time. It occurred to me then, responsible young man that I was, that we would need some means to awaken ourselves for our first day of training. When I asked my squad leader about it, he smiled and said I didn't need to worry about it. How nice.

Early the next morning, the door to my room slammed open. As I bolted out of a sound sleep, I became vaguely aware that a screaming banshee in the form of an upper-class cadet was shouting at me that I was "already late"!

My first cogent thought as I rose from the depths of sleep was a simple question: *If I'm already late, why didn't you get me up earlier?*

That event set up my next three and a half years at the Air Force Academy. The phrase "door slamming open" *sounds* like it should be an opportunity presenting itself. But it certainly didn't feel that way to me.

Many young men and women thrive in the environment of the military academies. I wasn't one of them.

AT THE AIR FORCE ACADEMY, built on a rocky plateau above seven thousand feet in the eastern shadow of the Rocky Mountains, winters can be long and bleak. The cadets speak of the period after the holidays and before spring break as the "Dark Ages."

Imagine life as a freshman at the Air Force Academy during the first winter there. Freshmen, or "doolies" (from the Greek word for "slave"), live dramatically restricted lives. Every waking moment is directed. Rather than amble to class at their leisure like other college students, doolies march at attention along specified concrete paths. They're subject to being stopped at any time and quizzed about arcana that they are required to memorize daily. Even the air they breathe is scarce and antagonistic in the winter. It's frigid, filled with ice fog.

The sun itself is not much help. On those days when it does come out, it seems to have just peeked over the eastern horizon when it begins to sink again behind the snow-laden Rocky Mountains, causing darkness to descend heavily on the school. The warmth of the Christmas season is a memory, and the mid-semester break will be long in coming.

This is not to say that nothing good happens in the depths of winter there. Just that it often seems that way.

I'd grown up in the warmth of the Deep South. We had long summers—not long winters. We had dogwoods and azaleas. Tall trees. Green grass.

The high plains desert to the east of the Academy and the rocky crags to the west each have their own stark beauty. But I wasn't seeing it. To me, it was as if all year, every year, was the Dark Ages. It was cold. The campus was sterile with its plain metal buildings and sharp edges. I was a less-than-sterling student, seriously challenged by the curriculum.

On top of all that, the institution went out of its way to provide door-slamming-open "non-opportunities," and I never really understood why. Even in the summertime, I wandered the campus in a haze of apparently meaningless rules that kept me looking over my shoulder, just waiting for the next banshee to come screaming into my world. In rare instances of quiet, I often wondered why I was choosing to put up with all this contrived adversity. Sometimes even now I marvel that I stayed.

A light appears through the mist…

WHAT, THEN, WAS GOING ON?

First, despite the oppression inherent in the Air Force Academy agenda, Fortune had put something in it to sustain me. Even there, even in the harshest of seasons, I had music.

I relish my memories of sitting in the chapel, lights sparkling brightly as they do in winter, keeping the Dark

Ages at bay, while the combined choirs of the Academy and Loretto Heights Women's College performed Handel's *Messiah*. I soon found myself singing in not one, but two musical groups, traveling around the country with both a chapel choir and the Cadet Chorale.

Could Fortune have been using the stark contrast between the bleakness of the Academy and the richness of singing to reveal something to me as I began my journey into adulthood? Was she trying to show me that even in the darkest of ages, I would still find lights? And that for me, those lights would always involve music?

Second, and on a far grander scale, I think she was giving me the chance to understand that doors slamming open can be far more significant than the banshees they usher in. I just had to be convinced to stick around long enough to recognize it. There was the *real* opportunity. Sometimes the good stuff coming down the road doesn't show up for a while. The Academy environment was teaching me how to persevere!

A stroke of luck—and a pen.

EARLY IN MY SENIOR YEAR, something happened for which I cannot account to this day. In a blazing and rare instance of foresight, the Air Force bureaucracy recognized that seven years into the future, they were going to be short of pilots. And if forced to choose, the number of bodies in cockpits was going to be more important than perfect vision.

So they changed the rules.

And quicker than you could execute an aileron roll in an F-22 Raptor, pretty much anybody in my class—and only my class of 1982—who could fog a mirror was now eligible to enter flight school. Just like that, my previously less-than-standard visual acuity was no factor in my potential to fly. I was now on track to become a pilot!

Here's perhaps the most remarkable thing: I had been a year late in entering the Academy. Though qualified, I had not been admitted immediately after high school because the class of 1981 had filled up before my application was processed. Apparently, then—despite my deep disappointment at the time—Fortune had placed me in the right place at exactly the right time to have a flying career!

Key Note

**Some realities are out of our hands—
that's not a bad thing.**

It took nearly four years, but the Wheel that had turned down so dramatically on that first morning at the Academy had finally started upward again as I entered the program to become a military pilot. That one stroke of "Fortune" opened many doors. And as suddenly as that dorm room door had blasted open on my first day at the Academy, real and obvious opportunity (no banshees required!) blasted into my life. A brass ring—at last, something meaningful to reach for—began to materialize where none had been before.

So what had driven me to remain during those long, long Dark Ages? Maybe it was stubbornness; perhaps a desire to win. Maybe I recognized in my heart of hearts that the Academy had real value to offer that I simply was not seeing.

What I do know is that had I not been in the class of 1982, or had I left the Academy prior to graduation, I would not have become a military pilot—my first brass ring. Had I not become a military pilot, I would likely not have become an airline pilot—my next brass ring.

And had I not remained at the Academy, I would not have benefited from the tremendous musical learning experiences that I received there. Might I have enjoyed similar growth elsewhere? Perhaps. But the specific understanding the Academy provided was foundational in the manifestation of my musical passion many years later.

It's interesting, isn't it, looking back and seeing embryonic perceptions from our youth of how life works? While I was busy looking over my shoulder, watching for those banshees, trying to decide whether to resign from the Academy or stick it out, I didn't fully comprehend the value of persevering. All I knew at the time was that I had a visceral need to do so.

Only later would I realize the pivotal role that perseverance would play in any success I would have in life. And that it was a skill the Academy had brought to me unseen during those "Dark Ages."

What Is *Your* Story So Far?

In your own past, you've had unpleasant door-slamming-open moments that ushered banshees and their shrieks into your life, rather than hoped-for opportunities. When have they occurred? Have those banshees dragged you into a period of darkness? Have they stopped your progress toward your brass rings?

Have you at times been able to see that the banshees screaming into your reality have been part of a larger picture? That they helped you grow or change in some way to prepare you for the opportunities that lay ahead?

Have you seen how those doors slamming open have advanced you toward long-term opportunities—lights once scarcely visible through the fog?

Today, are you taking advantage of open doors to stay engaged with your passion, still reaching for the brass rings you've described for yourself, whether or not they involve your livelihood? Or, are you, as I was at the Academy, still waiting for your brass rings to materialize?

Conductor's Notes

The Wheel turns. We sometimes get surprises when it does. Those doors *may* be slamming open to opportunity, though what comes through them may look unpleasant at the time. How we respond makes all the difference.

Now is the time to decide how to spend our years. What do you need to do to make your current orchestra into what you want it to be? Whom do you want to recruit to play your music? Where will you find them? What kind of music will you play?

We can use our surroundings to collect resources that will become useful later. When we're open to knowing how we should spend our resources, Fortune shows us the brass ring.

On June 2, 1982, I walked across the stage in Falcon Stadium and received my diploma and the congratulations of Vice President George H.W. Bush. A few hours later, I took a last look at the U.S. Air Force Academy in my rearview mirror and quietly celebrated the end of those particular Dark Ages.

*"I will study and prepare,
and perhaps my chance will come."*

—Abraham Lincoln

Chapter 2

It Isn't Always About You

LONG BEFORE MY EXPERIENCES at the USAF Academy, I decided to try out for drum major of my high school band. I'd had just enough exposure to conducting music in other venues to create a pull in that direction—a pull that would later become the single largest motivator of my entire life.

The audition for drum major required candidates to come up with a two-minute routine suitable for leading a marching band out onto a football field and then to demonstrate an ability to command through various vocal and physical gestures and maneuvers.

Four candidates were in the running: two would be selected as co–drum majors. The judging panel consisted of the high school band teacher, the junior high school band teacher, and the two current drum majors.

It Isn't Always About You

As the audition progressed, it became quite clear that one of the four candidates wasn't serious. His routine was weak and uncreative, and he made only a token attempt at the other audition checkpoints.

I was next in the barrel, and ready. *I'd* worked hard on *my* routine and thought it quite creative. *I* was bold with *my* vocal commands. *My* other required gestures were clear and decisive.

When the audition was done, I felt good. I didn't feel like *I'd* made a single mistake, and I was confident that *I* could beat out at least one of the remaining candidates.

As the other two candidates went through their auditions, nothing happened to change my mind. I continued to feel that *my* audition was competitive with each, and in my own still young and self-centered mind, *I* could see good reasons why *I* should be the first choice of the judges.

I was wrong.

> *A man said to the Universe:*
> *"Sir, I exist!"*
> *"However," replied the Universe,*
> *"The fact has not created in me*
> *A sense of obligation."*
>
> —Stephen Crane,
> *War Is Kind*

The last two candidates were selected.

And here was my introduction to the adult reality of the world as it *is* rather than how I might want it to be.

What I had failed to take into account was that this event was occurring in small-town Georgia in 1976. Seismic changes were underway that were not yet fully formed in the consciousness of our community, much less my own mind. The high school band teacher wanted to be seen as progressive, as one of the agents ushering these changes into our student world. And my personal demographic did not represent "change."

Of course, in *my* mind, *I* had performed perfectly. Thirty years later, my adult mind realizes that just maybe *I* was not an impartial observer and *I* may not have done as well as *I'd* thought. Without any recording of the events, I can never know with certainty.

What I can know, however, is that the world operates according to its own agenda—which, I have learned, *isn't all about me.*

It's something we "grown-ups" smile about now when we see it in our kids. Sure, the disappointments are bitter pills. I had wanted badly to be drum major, and *I* had done the work to prepare and had performed well during the audition. If competency were the only deciding criterion, as in a perfect world (at least in *my* perfect world), *I* probably would have won the day. It didn't work out that way.

And the world did not stop spinning.

What a great lesson for a teenage boy to learn! Sometimes you get what you try for; sometimes you don't.

It Isn't Always About You

Maybe it's time to examine the process! We try, we fail, we try again.

In this case, I'd previously tasted the positive energy of directing a musical organization. And being drum major was my first shot at getting to lead a high-energy musical group on a regular basis. I wanted that. And when it didn't happen, my simplistic, fiery teenage mind concluded that *I* had been cheated out of the opportunity by what would later be known as political correctness.

The experience left such a bad taste in my mouth that I was tempted to walk away from the whole idea of learning to be a conductor.

Thankfully I didn't. Instead, *I* got over it.

The lesson learned is so fundamental that it bears repeating:

Key Note

My wanting something does not create in the Universe a sense of obligation. Indeed, what goes on in this world isn't always about me.

So we stay in the process.

EVEN SO, FORTUNE OFTEN DOES BRING US what we *really* want. At the Air Force Academy, for instance, the privilege of directing the Protestant Chapel Choir—if only for short bits of the service—came my way on occasion. And I had other small chances to keep my hand in conducting over the years.

Of course, none of those little tastes, mere snippets really, were truly satisfying. They all felt like steps along the way to the real thing. And the problem with Fortune is that she reserves the right to go over the river, through the woods, and stop for a cup of tea at Grandma's house before bringing the package to our door. Which is why more than seven years after leaving the Academy, I still hadn't gotten my "big break."

Finally, though, one night in December of 1989, my moment arrived.

The church I attended and sang with in those years had a tradition of producing a large theatrical presentation as part of its yearly Christmas celebration. It was a montage of original drama written by the pastor, accompanied by a seventy-voice choir and a thirty-piece orchestra. The production usually ran for several evenings during the Christmas season, and this year was no exception. We would have four performances, Thursday evening through Sunday afternoon.

During a dramatic interlude in Wednesday evening's dress rehearsal, the musical director approached me and asked a couple of vague questions about whether I'd ever done any conducting.

I was completely unprepared for that.

With the rehearsal rolling right along, I didn't have time to give a lengthy response or to probe more deeply into what he was asking. So because I hadn't done any *major* conducting—nothing like the productions in his world—the best response I could come up with on the hop was "Well...not really." He nodded and went on about managing the rehearsal.

Almost as soon as that puzzling exchange was finished, the reason behind it became clear. Our conductor was only filling in at the church on an interim basis. And as his "day job," he was the music department head at a major university. I heard one of the other choir members laughing about how the university choir was scheduled for a Christmas concert at the same time as our Friday evening production. Somehow that detail had been overlooked, and our director was obliged to be in two places at once. He needed someone to handle the church concert so he could be at the university!

> "...and perhaps my chance will come."
> —Abraham Lincoln

Without waiting to hear another word, I left the choir and spent the remainder of the evening standing behind the director, watching over his shoulder as he conducted the singers and orchestra to the end of the show.

When rehearsal ended, I let him know that I had learned of his dilemma.

"I'm your man," I told him. "I can do this."

But he demurred.

The Symphony of Your Life / Mark Hardcastle

As the musicians filed out of the auditorium, the director explained that this was a major production and we were dealing with a professional orchestra. There simply wasn't much time to prepare. In fact, he said, it was so late that he was embarrassed to ask even his professional colleagues, whom he knew to be able and available, to step in.

"It's okay." I insisted. "I really can do this."

"No," he insisted in turn. Late as it was, he'd find a professional musician and wouldn't set me up for failure. We were friends, after all, and he didn't want me to be embarrassed.

I reached out to touch the director's arm. I looked straight into his eyes, and one more time I repeated: "I can do this."

The director paused. He locked into my gaze for what felt like an eternity…and then he handed me his baton.

The room was empty, the choir and orchestra gone for the night. He invited me to stand on the podium. Turning toward the front of the auditorium, he pointed to where the musicians had been and would be the following evening. "There's the orchestra," he said. "Here's the sheet music for one of the production numbers. You know this piece. Start 'em off."

I opened the music, raised the baton before the imaginary orchestra and choir, and began to conduct the piece. I progressed through only four measures—a very brief sixteen beats—before the director stopped me.

"You're right, Mark. You can do this. Here's the music for the part of the production you'll need to conduct. Be in my office at noon tomorrow and we'll talk it through."

My preparation consisted of staying up very late that night studying the scores, spending an hour the next day in his office—during which he briefed me on "little agreements I've made with the orchestra that aren't written on the music"—and then studying his direction from my place in the choir during the opening night production Thursday evening.

During Friday night's performance, while the stage was dark during a scene change, I slipped out of the choir and down the aisle to the front of the church. I sat down beside the director and once again he passed me his baton. Then we wished each other well, and he rose and left, trusting the production to my hands.

Within seconds, the lights came up for the next number and I took my place on the podium. The orchestra, having been prepped beforehand, looked up, ready for their cue. The choir, however, was completely surprised. Who was this clean-shaven guy in a pinstriped Victorian caroler's tuxedo? Where was the fully bearded director in white tie and tails? What had happened during the blackout?

I gave the orchestra the downbeat and we were off and running. As the vocal entry approached in the music, I sensed indecision from the choir; they were clearly wondering whether this "unknown" director would be able to bring them in.

Then, right before their entrance, the choir recognized me. I felt them mentally ask across the space separating us: *"Mark—can you do this?"*

For an answer, I brought them in *exactly* as they'd rehearsed. And when they realized that "Yes! You absolutely can do this!" the burst of energy they released my way was palpable down to my very soul.

That moment was a full twenty years ago and I still see and feel it as if it were yesterday. The remainder of the production went off without a hitch. And my breath still catches when I think of that night.

THE CHRISTMAS STORY would not be complete without the retelling of The Magnificat. Reflecting on the blessed event, Mary, the Virgin Mother of Jesus, wonders at all that is happening in her young life. "My soul magnifies the Lord," she exclaims, "for He has done great things!"

Indeed, this tender moment was conveyed through a soprano aria in our production. And after my first time on a podium with a real orchestra and a real choir, producing a Christmas story of our own, I repeated The Magnificat to myself. In my little world, something great had happened beyond what I had known to be possible. Before then, it was a dream. An ethereal mist. Something to be pursued but not yet within my grasp. From that night on, it was real.

The next night, during the choir warm-ups before the concert, the regular director/professor/composer quieted the singers and thanked me in front of everyone for stepping in. And then, for a third time, he presented me with his baton—the baton with which he had started the concert and I had completed it—as a token of gratitude. I still treasure this gift as a memento of a grand occasion, and have enjoyed using it before choirs in the years that have followed.

I must conduct!

ONE OF THE GREAT THINGS about being human is that we get to have rare and profound experiences. Conducting the Christmas production was one of those for me. When the choir responded to my baton, I knew instantly that this was my calling.

I am a conductor. I must conduct. And the rest of my life will be spent looking for opportunities to recapture the intensity of that first concert.

The year that followed was a year of musical joy. After the success of the Christmas production, the director made me his protégé. His university duties necessarily took priority over church activities and sometimes required him to be away. On those occasions, he entrusted me with the weekly worship services, which included both directing the choir and leading the congregation in song.

Similarly, because of his position as a music professor, he was often asked to help out with special musical productions around town. He received far more requests than he could possibly honor and was known to pass them on to me when he thought it appropriate.

Those opportunities, both within the church and outside of it, formed me into a true conductor. And each one served to consolidate the musical foundation that would prepare me for even greater opportunities down the road.

What's Your Response?

Have there been times in your life when you've been chest-stabbed by injustice? Has some form of discrimination taken from you what was rightfully yours? Has someone else received the promotion you deserved? Someone else won the trophy you had earned?

Really? Are you sure about that?

Well, maybe. But here's the bottom line: You're still here to tell the tale. And think back: What did you do to get beyond that particular crisis? How have you redefined that situation, that process, to make yourself stronger, better, and more determined to succeed in your own Yin-Yang universe? What do your new goals look like since that situation has receded? Are you still looking for opportunities to pursue your passions in spite of how others have advanced themselves or been advanced at your expense?

And then there was my daughter…

BACK WHEN ANNA WAS SMALL, she and I went to Boettcher Concert Hall in Denver for a concert presented by three of the cast members of the Disney film *The Little Mermaid*. Anna, like many other girls born in the early nineties, was enamored of Ariel. She could not wait to see Jodi Benson in person. And she wasn't disappointed! It was a wonderful performance, filled with every possible delight for a little girl. But the final curtain wasn't the end of the show.

After the concert, Ms. Benson graciously stood in the lobby to greet her young fans. Anna was totally taken with *actually speaking* to the character who'd voiced Ariel. It was an exceptional night for all of us!

Fast-forward a few years. When Anna was eight, she was invited to join the Colorado Children's Chorale. In due course, she sang her first concert with them at Boettcher Hall, and she was more excited than most because she remembered Jodi Benson performing on that very stage. It was a moment of wonder for her. Little second-grade Anna, following in Jodi Benson's footsteps: "I may even breathe some of the same air!" Yup, she actually said that!

Fast-forward again, through all the performance training with the Children's Chorale and two Colorado All-State Choir experiences, and we see Anna as a young lady brimming with unrealized ambition to star in musicals on Broadway. She knew what she wanted to do and was determined to learn how to do it.

As part of that process, Anna attended audition after audition with both community theater companies and her high school drama club, looking forward to the day when she'd earn her first lead role. But that elusive lead was always one other singer/actor away. She always ended up in the chorus.

One might be forgiven for concluding that musical theater just wasn't Anna's thing after all. Maybe she really *didn't* have the chops. Maybe her singing, dancing, and acting were truly not good enough to land a leading role in a major production. But one would be wrong.

On September 1st of 2009, all of that changed.

That fall, Anna found herself as a freshman at a well-endowed community college in Wyoming with a scholarship to study musical theater. Because the college was in a small town, its theater was a cultural center for the area and the department's productions were always well attended. One of Anna's first major challenges was an audition for a part in Gershwin's *Crazy for You,* which would be presented to the community at the end of the semester. And finally, after all those gigs as part of the chorus, Anna won the role of Polly Baker, the female lead.

Of course, Anna was over the moon. So was I! A father dreams with his little girl and their hearts ache together when the inevitable disappointments happen. But when the victories come, the joys are shared as well. And the chance to see Anna on stage, in a leading role at last, was a special joy for me!

It Isn't Always About You

As I stood in the lobby on opening night, Anna texted from backstage to ask where I'd be sitting. Not thinking much of it, I responded with my seat location and then entered the auditorium to settle in for the show.

The reason for Anna's question became apparent as she prepared to sing one of the show's early numbers. She casually strolled across the stage to where she could look right at me, and then belted out the iconic song "Someone to Watch Over Me."

Imagine! My Anna on stage in her first lead role singing that. To me! As she crooned about *somebody I'm longing to see…to my heart he carries the key…*my *own* heart nearly came out of my chest.

A better writer would be able to convey the full mixture of emotions I felt—the joy, the love, the vicarious success. But when I try, the page just gets covered in hyperbole and cliché. Suffice it to say that was another night of treasure that I'll be able to enjoy for the rest of my life.

Now, all of that would have been beyond good enough. But having Anna in this particular role had a special twist. The show *Crazy for You* had premiered on Broadway on February 19, 1992, and had run for 1,622 performances over four years, winning a Tony Award for Best Musical along the way. And during this successful stint on Broadway, the role of Polly Baker had been played by…

Wait for it…

Jodi Benson!

So, through Polly Baker, Anna got to do more than just "breathe the same air" as her childhood hero. She got to actually be her hero, Jodi Benson, for two weeks that October.

And so it went. Success followed success for Anna in those two years with that college. They included more lead roles as large as Maria in *The Sound of Music,* as well as other smaller roles along the way.

But what if Anna had given up after high school? What if she'd never auditioned for *Crazy for You* at college?

The lesson remains:

Key Note

Stay in the process.

Had Anna *not* stayed in the process—had she elected not to persevere through all those "failed" auditions over all those years—her dream would have died and her life today would be different indeed.

So where is she now? Anna is again a scholarship student in musical theater, this time at the American Musical and Dramatic Academy in New York City. She walks by Lincoln Center every day on her way to class. Her teachers are active participants in current Broadway shows. She is developing her craft in the heart of the theater world with people who are "doing it." Her perseverance and determination have landed her on the doorstep of her dreams, and we foresee great things for her as she makes those dreams real.

Conductor's Notes

We live in the world as it is, not necessarily as we'd like it to be.

It really isn't all about us.

Fortune provides opportunity—we provide results.

Do you know yet what it is that you "must do"? Will you recognize the podium when Fortune offers it to you? Have you decided how you'd use the baton on the table before you in an ideal world?

It Isn't Always About You

ANNA WILL NEVER FORGET the many disappointments of looking at the cast sheets and seeing her name among the chorus members time after time. Nor will I ever forget the sting of realizing that *I* wasn't going to be the drum major of my high school band. The good news is that Anna and I moved on quickly after each disappointment. The result was that we were able to receive the opportunities Fortune had set up for us later in life.

The memories created during my short tenure as associate musician, for instance, are riches that can never be taken away. They are some of those bright lights that sustain me when my Wheel starts to turn down.

And the year spent developing my new craft was not only one of great joy, but also one of great growth. I learned lessons about conducting, composing, and musical concepts at a remarkable rate and depth. At the end of the year when the time came for me to leave that church to start another chapter in my life, I fully expected to continue that growth and somehow to put those lessons to work. But Fortune had something else in mind for me. She spun her Wheel, and I set my baton aside for longer than I would have imagined.

It would take nearly ten years. But when it was time to pick up the baton again, the lessons learned in that unique set of circumstances came back quickly and served me well.

For all of that, *I* am deeply grateful.

"If one advances confidently in the direction of his dreams, and endeavors to live the life which he has imagined, he will meet with success unexpected in common hours."

—Henry David Thoreau

Chapter 3

The Power of One

WHAT, THEN, WAS FORTUNE'S PLAN? She chose this point in my life to set some great shifts into motion. Was she just being fickle? It seemed that way. Why these changes, and why now?

My time at the top of the Wheel had been deeply satisfying. And I had achieved some great things, at least in my own little world. Maybe that was the point. I had completed a growth cycle. I had reigned for a season. Was it time for me to do some more growing? Was this the beginning of a completely new cycle?

Events certainly made me feel that my Wheel was starting down again.

First, the pastor finally found a full-time church musician. As was appropriate, the composer/conductor/

professor relinquished his role at the church, and my time of learning-by-doing in that setting came to a close.

The circumstances of my flying life shifted as well, pulling me away from the military and toward the world of commercial aviation.

Change was indeed in the wind. A new cycle was establishing itself. It was time for me to decrease my focus on music and concentrate on getting hired by an airline.

A job search would, of course, involve résumés and interviews, licensing exams, physical exams, and simulator tests. So I hired the résumé writers, bought the study guides, began the process of commercial licensing, and started asking anybody who knew anything about the airline hiring process for intelligence to help me prepare for my interviews.

The flurry of applications went out to all the major carriers of the day, and thankfully I received invitations to interview at several of them.

This story is about my interview at the company I ultimately joined and for which I still fly today.

I arrived at the airline's human resources office at the appointed hour and was greeted by two interviewers. One was a human resources representative; the other, an active captain. The captain's job was to ask technical flying questions to validate my experience and to get an impression of my judgment as a pilot. The HR rep's job was much more subjective. She was tasked with evaluating my thought processes and determining whether I'd be a good fit for the company culture.

The interview was intense. It lasted almost ninety minutes and consisted of questions designed to get beyond any candidate's prepared responses. I was confident of my answers to all the objective questions posed by the captain, and I felt pretty good about my responses to the far more ambiguous queries from the HR rep. All in all, I was satisfied with my performance, and while anxious to know the outcome, I knew I'd forever sleep well knowing I'd been prepared and had given it a good shot.

In due course, a letter arrived in the mail that all aspiring commercial pilots hope one day to receive: an offer of employment at the airline of my choice. Over the next few months, I completed my obligations to the United States Air Force, became a civilian, and reported to the airline to begin my new career.

The grass was indeed greener on the other side of the fence. My first two years as an airline pilot were "such stuff as dreams are made on" (with thanks to The Bard). The pay was great and the working conditions better than I had ever experienced in the Air Force. My home life was great. I was living a charmed life.

What I didn't know was how close I had come to never receiving that letter.

PRIOR TO ANY COMMERCIAL FLIGHT, it's not unusual for one of the pilots to make an announcement welcoming the

The Power of One

passengers on board. We give a bit of information about the flight time, weather at the destination, and anything interesting about the flight route for those who might enjoy looking out the window along the way. During this welcome, we also routinely introduce ourselves and our crewmembers by name.

One day, after I'd been flying commercially for nearly a decade, I had just completed the usual pre-flight broadcast when a gentleman entered the cockpit and introduced himself. He was the captain who had interviewed me all those years prior. To my utter amazement, with all the interviews he'd conducted, he remembered me. Upon hearing my name over the PA, he'd decided to come up and tell me the rest of the story.

After each pilot interview, the process called for the two interviewers to compare notes and make a recommendation to the human resources manager as to whether they thought the candidate should be hired. In my case, the HR rep went first. She had not been nearly as impressed with my performance as I had imagined. In fact, her initial response was something like: "I'm gonna shoot him down."

The captain, however, had been beyond well-pleased. He was inclined to hire me on the spot and couldn't imagine her wanting to send me packing.

According to the captain, the rep had no concrete justification for her position. She couldn't point to anything specific she didn't like about my answers. She had only a vague impression that I was somehow incompatible with "her" airline.

At that point, the captain lost it. Here, he argued, was an opportunity to hire a highly experienced military pilot with thousands of hours in the air—a couple hundred of which were in combat defending *his* country during the recent Persian Gulf War—who had given perfectly satisfactory answers to every question posed by either of the interviewers. And now this HR bureaucrat had the gall to reject him for no reason she could clearly explain.

With that, the captain took it upon himself to give the rep an ultimatum: She was going to join him in giving this pilot a "definitely hire" recommendation or the captain was going to resign from the interview group and was going to make sure that all the hiring supervisors understood why.

What?!

Obviously, the HR rep backed down and I was hired.

Key Note

Even when it's not all about you, the outcome can be good.

The Power of One

What a stunning revelation! I was speechless. I'm sure I stuttered out some sort of inadequate thanks for the risk the captain had taken on my behalf. But before I could recover from my shock and thank him properly, he had returned to his seat.

Since then, I've liked to think that the captain was right in his judgment. To date, I've worked well and faithfully in the service of that same airline for the better part of two decades. I have flown thousands of flights without incident, taking satisfied customers where they need to go. In the process of logging tens of thousands of flight hours, I've helped people experience life, taking them to weddings, funerals, business meetings, and resort vacations. In that way, I've touched the periphery of hundreds of thousands of lives.

Nevertheless, on so many levels, my interview that day *wasn't* about me. The HR rep had her feelings about "her" airline. Her emotional judgments were really about her. And the captain was obviously fed up with the system; his frustration was about him. Still, I am grateful to that captain for taking the stand he did. And for the almost mystical way that the mindsets of everyone involved, combined with the internal politics of the airline's hiring department, all worked together to give my Wheel a huge push in the right direction.

Which led me to wonder again: *Was* Fortune being fickle, inciting all that change back at the church? It *had* felt like my Wheel of Fortune was pitching over, sending me down from the top.

Regardless of Fortune's intent, all that turmoil simply set me up for a different kind of success. Remembering how that new cycle began—with a seemingly unpleasant set of circumstances—has helped me keep a more balanced perspective when other challenges have come my way. These days, I'm less inclined to panic when those Dark Ages start to set in. In fact, looking back on situations like this enables me to look ahead with hope, if not true excitement, about what rings will be within my grasp the next time I hit the top!

Whose Wheels Have Turned with Yours?

Remember a few pages back when we talked about those times you felt "chest-stabbed by injustice"? Well, if we're honest, we should pause here to look at the other side of the coin.

Admit it. You've also had times in life when you got a break. Sometimes you knew it. Sometimes it didn't become apparent for quite a while. But someone did something outside your understanding that made a huge difference in your experience on this planet. Thinking back, what did that look like? Did someone bring the brass ring closer to you? Did they advance you around the Wheel?

Better yet, have you made a similar impact in the life of someone else? Have you quietly helped someone to whom you owed nothing move closer to his or her dream?

Is it possible for us to be vigilant so we see such opportunities when they arise?

Conductor's Notes

All "luck" isn't bad. Being prepared helps, but it isn't necessarily the controlling factor.

When Fortune smiles, you may not know it at the time.

Because Fortune has used others along our way, we should be willing to allow Fortune to use us for the benefit of others.

Are you recruiting band members to whom you can be a mentor? As you interview prospects, are you guarding against unnecessary "standards" that create ill will and are ultimately counterproductive? In building your orchestra, are you building relationships that benefit the musical community as a whole?

The Power of One

MY AIRLINE CAREER almost never happened. Thanks to the fortitude of one man who stood up to his opposition, I was given an opportunity that would otherwise have been denied. And I had no idea that this battle had even taken place. Incredible!

"Make no small plans,
for they have not the power to stir men's blood."

—Niccolo Machiavelli

Chapter 4

Be the Spark

MY NEW CAREER was off and running. Before I knew it, I was living in another city and had three kids who were growing like weeds.

As the story picks up, my oldest son was attending fifth grade within a private school system. The musical organization was such that the elementary school had its own band instructor, while the middle and high school bands were led by a second teacher.

So there we were one spring evening to listen to my son's band concert. All three schools were included in the program.

My son's group opened the concert, and of course, they sounded how you'd expect an elementary school band to sound: very elementary!

In due course, they were followed by the middle school band. I became slightly concerned when I realized that the middle school group, too, sounded about how you'd expect an elementary school band to sound.

My concern grew into alarm when the high school band played, and even this most advanced group didn't play much differently than the fifth-grade students. Clearly something was wrong. What was it?

And was there a way for me to help?

As the new term got underway the following autumn, I approached the band instructor with an offer to volunteer in her high school classroom. My intent was to take on the separate rehearsals with various instrument sections as needed, which would allow her to leverage her class time with the full band.

The teacher was happy to have me on board, and before I knew it, she had made me a guest conductor. As a reward for helping out, I would be allowed to conduct the full band for one of the five pieces on the upcoming program.

How exciting, but challenging. Would my presence help or hinder? What really needed to be done?

Once we hit our stride, details about the situation began to emerge. The band teacher was a fine individual and certainly loved music. And through the sheer strength of her will, she had maintained the school's band program well enough for it to stand on its own. But something *was* missing. And I was starting to understand what it was.

It's the spark!

I WATCHED THE REHEARSALS for several weeks. The kids ran through the same warm-up exercises day after day and then went through the agenda, receiving very little in the way of musical instruction. And all at once I knew: The teacher had lost her passion. This had become little more than a duty to her, and that sense of routine was being conveyed to the students.

It didn't help that most of these kids were not in the band by choice; they were there because their parents required it of them. So they came to class, blew on their horns, endured the hour, and left the room as quickly as they could, day in and day out.

My heart went out to this teacher. By now I knew how impressive it was for her to be in the position she was in at all. She had confided that her own musical background was unremarkable and that she had never known the joy and privilege of being in any high-level musical organization.

The result was that she was struggling. She had a heart for music and a basic technical understanding, but she simply did not have the depth of training to enable her to convey the nuances of great music to her students.

So how could I help? On paper, my own musical education had been no better. I had no music degree. But what I lacked in college-level coursework, I made up for in experience under great teachers, going all the way back to my high school years. In other words, I'd had the great "fortune" of having done the things we both wanted to teach these kids to do. My enthusiasm and ability to talk about the expressive aspects of music could be a great complement to this teacher's more technical and organizational skill set. I had what she didn't have, and vice versa. What a great setup!

Neither of us could get it done alone, but together we could accomplish something special.

Key Note

Be the spark.

So the question became: *How can I show this group of students that there is far more to playing an instrument than simply blowing air through it? That as musicians, they are the vehicles through which a composer conveys a message to an audience? That by transforming the notes from the page into meaningful music for a listener, the musicians themselves can be transformed?*

As high school band students, they should have learned this already. They should have been in a position to study and hone their craft. They should have been working to get better at presenting the composer's message to those who would listen.

But they hadn't a clue.

By the time the first concert came around in late fall, I, at least, was in my element—conducting sectional rehearsals and, once a week or so, rehearsing my one piece with the entire band. Never, in any other time or place, had I enjoyed my "work" more. But were the kids getting it? It was hard to say.

And the clock was ticking. I was there completely at the pleasure of the regular teacher, and she could withdraw her invitation at any time. So it had to be full throttle for whatever window of opportunity was available to me.

Each day, I pulled at least one instrument section into a small rehearsal room to work on some specific passages of music in which I could point out what the composer was trying to do. I showed the brass section how rising notes could convey excitement; the woodwinds learned how playing softer or slower encourages contemplation. Those playing instruments with higher ranges learned how to introduce whimsy to a piece.

When I wasn't working on sectional rehearsals, I made a point of moving among the students so I could show the lower voices where the composer was using them to create a sense of continuity and steadiness. Or where the percussion players could instantly change the direction of the piece, simply by moving accents to different beats within a measure.

And, of course, I was given time to rehearse the band as a whole for "my" piece in the concert. This gave us a chance to weave together everything I'd taught them and use all these new musical elements to create a story.

Was it working?

The first inkling of my impact came the night of the first concert. It was too soon for the performance to be anything other than musically miserable—but this time it was entirely enthusiastic. The kids came to life when we played together. They noticed it themselves, and their parents noticed as well. (Just the usual niceties came my way the night of concert, but soon after, the parent network started to buzz about how differently the kids had played under my baton!)

This concert brought my entire being to life with the same sensations I had felt in that church a decade before. This was what I was meant to do!

But a moment of truth arrived as the kids packed up their instruments in the band room after the concert. As they filed out, I congratulated them one by one on their success of the evening.

And then one asked me if I would be there tomorrow.

Pause.

I actually didn't know. My designated time had ended, and the teacher and I hadn't talked about extending it.

A shadow crossed over the student's face and he asked me to *please* come back tomorrow.

And then another student asked. And another.

It wasn't all of them, but enough. Enough that I knew that the message was getting through. The students *were* learning to go beyond just blowing air through their instruments. They *were* seeing and feeling that making music involves much more than merely playing notes!

But even that wasn't the *real* moment of truth. Just a few weeks later, I came down with acute appendicitis. My recovery from surgery kept me out of class for a full two weeks. The teacher was thoughtful enough to buy me a get-well card and pass it around the class for the students to sign.

That card very quickly became one of my most prized possessions. It said things like "Get well soon. It's not the same without you!" and "Come back quickly—you're our only hope!" If my home were ever to catch fire, I'd grab the family videos and photos, and then that card. Clearly, these kids were starting to understand. But there was more yet to do. Much more.

The Christmas concert that year was a joy. My students and I had established a rapport and were enjoying each other on a daily basis. They were learning about intonation, dynamics, tempo, and all the other musical elements that are the composer's tools. The kids were having fun as they picked up technique.

But something was *still* missing.

Be the Spark

ABOUT A MONTH INTO THE SECOND SEMESTER, the music teacher's baby got sick. She needed a few days off to care for her child. Though I was not certified as a substitute teacher, she and the school administration simply trusted me to take over. So for that brief period, I rehearsed not only sectionals and my one designated concert piece. For three consecutive days, I was *the* teacher.

As always, my teaching materials were the pieces of music for the upcoming concert. One was a tone poem based on the Old Testament stories of the Israelite captivity in Babylon. What lessons could it convey?

In three sections, the music evoked an image of what life might have been like during those times of slavery. The first section was up-tempo, calling to mind a bustling society of busy hands and productive lives, if not completely happy because of the slavery. The second section, while continuing the musical themes of the first, was deeply contemplative, taking the listener into the Israelite home during the Sabbath—a time of rest, family communion, and worship. The third movement repeated the first, as the family members returned to their weekly routines.

The themes of the first and third movements were lively and complex—fun for a musician to play. The middle restful, worshipful section, contained a soaring trumpet solo through which the composer might take the listener into the depths of the Israelite soul crying to God for freedom from the Babylonians.

The Symphony of Your Life / Mark Hardcastle

The class could discern the general context from the title of the piece and the scriptural notation that the composer had given. But who knows specifically what he had in mind? What I gave those young musicians was an idea. Some possibilities. And we worked on conveying those possibilities and others, for those three days. And I will never forget what happened as class came to an end on the third day.

It had been a particularly good rehearsal. The students had come to class prepared, open-minded, and feeling that something important was about to happen. We had worked with an unusual intensity to understand and communicate the message of the piece about the Israelite captivity. We were all deeply touched.

As class ended and the students put away their instruments, I sensed their imaginations taking them places they had never been before. Hardly a word was spoken, but as they filed past me on the way to the next hour's class, I could see it in their faces. Glowing. Eyes on fire. They understood.

My job was done.

> *"To everything there is a season."*
>
> —Solomon, King of Israel

The concert that followed was the last time I raised my baton—the very baton I had used during the long-ago Christmas production—for many, many years.

The day after that concert, the band teacher advised me that my time with the band was now complete. She offered no explanation. I can imagine, though, that she had also become aware of the parent murmurings about how the kids seemed to play differently when I was on the podium. While I could not possibly have taken over the teacher's position, I fear she may have been threatened by my presence. Which is a shame.

From my perspective, good things were happening all around. The teacher had me as a support system when she needed to be absent, and the kids were growing musically by leaps and bounds.

In the end, the band teacher did leave the school at the completion of that term. And as it happened, one of the most respected high school band teachers in the entire state was retiring from the public school system and agreed to fill the new opening at this private school as a second career.

The kids' progress did nothing but accelerate from that day forward.

Whose Wheel Can You Kick-Start?

    Here had been a chance for me to step into a situation of need and make an impact on lives. When have you seen such an opportunity to "turn someone else's Wheel"? Where is *your* band that you can teach to make music? Where is *your* band teacher with a sick child for whom you can step in and carry her load for a time?

    What talents do you have that may or may not be unique to you, but which you can use in some unique situation you are aware of? Where is there a need in your world that you can fill but about which you've been hesitant?

Conductor's Notes

Opportunities appear all around us if we'll take the time to notice.

The turning of our Wheels often affects the Wheels of those within our spheres.

We are capable. We can contribute to the lives of others. We should. We can advance toward our own brass rings in doing so.

While your own Symphony is not yet fully formed, there is another one in your sphere who needs your talents. Can you step in to help with sectional rehearsals? Do you have a specific talent that is absent in that particular orchestra?

WHEN I REMINISCE NOW about that night in the Christmas production and those concerts at the high school, I sometimes wonder about my own high school experience. What would my world have been like had I lost my ambition to become a conductor based on what I considered an unjust decision at my drum major audition? How much richer my life has been and will be for having held onto that dream! And maybe, just maybe, the lives of some young adults out there are a little richer because I was there to show them something about music.

For a season, I served the Universe as an airline pilot, taking people where they needed to go around the world. But I was still a conductor, looking for my next opportunity to conduct. I knew it would come in due time. And it did.

"Pa, he always said a man had to look spry for himself, because nobody would do it for him; your opportunities didn't come knocking around, you had to hunt them down and hog-tie them."

—Louis L'Amour,
Chancy

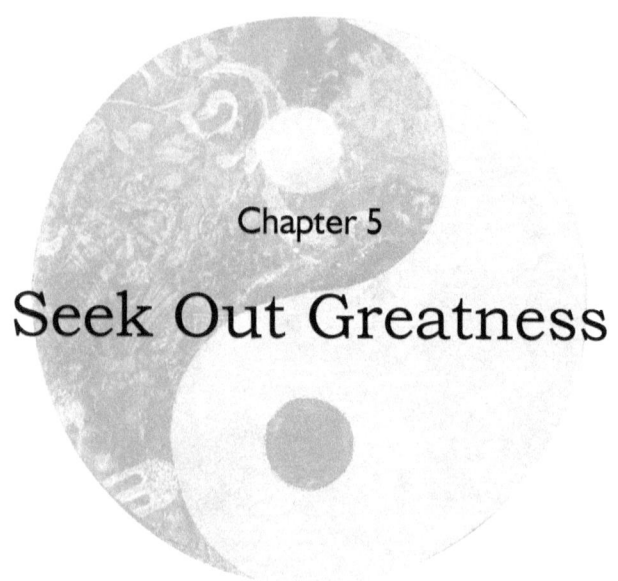

Chapter 5

Seek Out Greatness

THREE OF MY FOUR CHILDREN had the great fortune to be members of the Colorado Children's Chorale (CCC).

The CCC is an organization of musical excellence if ever there was one. Hundreds of children audition each year, as young as eight years old, and those who are successful progress through Prep, Apprentice, Concert, and ultimately to Regional and National Tour Choirs, before graduating at grade eight.

I have had the joy of watching my kids make that progression over the last twelve years, and my youngest is still in the Tour Choir.

FOR SEVERAL YEARS, the Chorale made it possible for one parent to conduct one piece at the spring concert. During my third child's final year, when it looked as though my association with the CCC was coming to a close, I was determined to grab that opportunity and make it mine.

And I did. Having been a "Chorale parent" for ten years, I knew who to call to get the ball rolling. I made those requisite calls, asked the necessary questions, learned the how-tos, did the paperwork, sent the emails, and in the end did whatever was necessary to make sure I was the one on the podium that year.

And, like that letter from the airline back in '91, an email arrived from the Chorale notifying me of my selection. I had done it! And I could not wait to get in front of this elite group with my baton.

At the very next rehearsal, on a Tuesday, the director of the Chorale introduced me to the group as this year's guest conductor and handed me my sheet music. The kids took a few minutes to familiarize me with the piece, and suddenly I had only two weeks to get ready!

Prepare!

Having not raised my baton before a musical group in seven years, I was a bit rusty. But I was fiendishly determined to put on a good show. The music was a very brief octavo—

maybe three minutes in length—but I put in hours before Thursday's rehearsal, when I'd be in front of the group, asking them to trust me to lead them to a great sound.

Thursday arrived. The director told me what to expect and ran me through the piece to check my ability level. We were both pleasantly surprised that I *did* seem prepared, and maybe, just maybe, knew a little about conducting!

So there I was—rehearsing that tremendous children's choir, with my son in the group before me. That alone would have been worth the years of waiting. But it was only the beginning.

Critique. Correct. Prepare some more!

Five days later, I was on stage at Boettcher Hall(!) with these kids in their concert tableau for the dress rehearsal. I had, of course, taken to heart all that I had learned at rehearsal the previous week; and with even further study, I had been able to apply those lessons to the music. Now here, on this day, I saw an inkling of the possible.

During practice, the notes had spoken quietly to me, and I had a better idea of what they were trying to say. But I had no opportunity to explain it to the kids with words; this was dress rehearsal. It was time to conduct.

Seek Out Greatness

Kids. But pros. This piece had been part of their repertoire for years, so they knew it intimately. That allowed them to focus on what was being asked of them. And they followed brilliantly. When I was clear with my direction, they gave me exactly what I wanted. When they didn't, I identified places in the music where I simply needed to be more precise.

It was obvious I still had more work to do. Even so, the kids seemed ready to accept me as part of their musical world.

Key Note

Call it "good," then be bold.

At some point, preparation ends and it's time to perform. At the end of rehearsal that day, the director had only a few words for me as we shifted our focus from practice to performance. She urged me to abandon the sheet music and give myself wholly to the kids. This would be a once-in-a-lifetime chance to connect with these fabulous individuals on a level only a handful of people would ever realize. I took her advice and spent the remaining days memorizing every note, every dynamic, every nuance of the piece.

When I was fully able to stand before the kids without the music in front of me, I called it good. It was time, and I was ready. My next interaction with the kids would be in concert, on stage, before the audience. With my baton in hand.

The same baton I had used in my last concert with the student band seven years before.

The same baton I had used at the Christmas Festival of Lights more than a decade before that.

Almost before I realized what was happening, I was in the wings awaiting my cue. The director gave me a gracious introduction, and with all the boldness I could muster, I walked across the stage and took my place on the podium. I paused to make sure I was completely present with the kids on stage. Then I raised my baton, locked eyes with the accompanist, and we set the piece in motion. He and I progressed as one until it was time for the kids to join us.

And as I had done with the church choir during that Christmas season, and as I had done with the high school band who played with all their hearts about the Israelites beside the waters of Babylon, I invited these children into the music.

And it happened again. The magic. The high. The point at which everything dissolves except the music and those who make it. I felt as if we were the only ones in the room. Just myself and those kids, speaking to each other across the space between us, giving our hearts to the Universe and the beauty we were creating together.

Seek Out Greatness

And so it was until the applause began, even as my magic wand suspended the final note. The crowd's response seemed almost an intrusion, though ultimately welcome—like being awakened from a strange and powerful dream by the aroma of bacon and coffee of a winter's morning.

As the ovation built, I gave the final cutoff. I thanked the kids and congratulated them on the wonder of what we had done. Then I turned to acknowledge the audience.

And I received the payoff.

It was as if Fortune was reminding me once again that good things could absolutely be mine. Her only question was whether or not I was willing to seek out those opportunities and resolve to grasp them. Getting to the stage in Boettcher Hall had been a monumental process. This day had been more than worth the effort.

What Is Your Passion?

What has the Universe been telling *you* for years? Where do you need to be? What is it that you must do to accomplish what you were placed here to accomplish? Have you distilled and defined your passion out of the vague sense of direction you've always felt? What does a life well-lived look like for you?

Conductor's Notes

Stop right now and take this chance to think about what you want out of life. Again, our time here is limited—how should we spend it?

Once you know, never stop moving toward the truest "you." Study, prepare, and look for your chance. Preparation trumps desire every time. When the Wheel brings you around to your opportunity, act with the boldness that preparation allows.

Right now you know of an opportunity to conduct. An orchestra exists that will allow you to step up. Don't be shy. It's not yours yet. But you will grow and learn as a result of the experience. Ultimately your own orchestra will be better for it.

The Symphony of Your Life / Mark Hardcastle

As I turned from the kids that day, I felt the energy of the audience on my face. Maybe it was merely the warmth of the stage lights, but I prefer to think it was the enchantment of the extraordinary music we had created together. Clearly, the kids and I had done what we came to do: continue the dialogue with the folks who had come to listen. I took my bow and moved off into the wings as the director returned to the stage and started the kids off on their grand finale.

And who knew when my next opportunity would arise? I had no idea. Of this I was certain, however: Once again, Fortune had taken pains to remind me that I am a conductor. And there is a place in that world for me.

"It's a funny thing that when a man hasn't anything on earth to worry about, he goes off and gets married."

—Robert Frost

Chapter 6

Live *Your* Best Life

WHEN I WAS YOUNGER, I imagined a sort of "life timetable" for at least my first several years of adulthood. I had an idea that I should finish college, get established in a career, and then get married and start having kids. It wasn't a particularly rigid plan, but it seemed to make sense in the grand scheme of things.

And as things go, that's pretty much the way my life fell together through my mid-twenties. After finishing my term at the USAF Academy, I entered the military as a pilot. Following a year of pilot training, I became an instructor pilot, teaching the syllabus I had myself only just completed. A year or so later, my career was well-enough established that I felt comfortable rebalancing my life to allow for a bit more social time.

And, sure enough, I met a girl who seemed to be a perfect match. I was a person of faith; so was she. I was ambitious; she was too. She and I were both in shape and enjoyed exercising. And she was very much into music and a good singer. Not only that, but she was academically accomplished with a master's degree, and she had been the president of her college sorority, making her a good social fit for a young officer in the U.S. military.

There was one problem, however: I wasn't emotionally hooked. Sure, I enjoyed her company. We had lots of fun together. But something seemed to be missing. Even though I liked her a great deal, I didn't have the feeling that I couldn't do without her. And on the long list of objective criteria I had set for myself in a potential mate was that one very subjective criterion: I had to feel like I couldn't live without her.

When the gut speaks, we should listen.

It was a bit of a dilemma. On paper, I couldn't imagine finding someone more compatible. And I certainly didn't want to give up on her without knowing that I was acting deliberately and with all the best thinking I could find.

Feeling the need for additional wisdom, I decided to seek advice from someone in a position of authority for just such questions. So I went to my pastor. His counsel, based on his personal experience and his having worked with dozens of couples over the years, was that Hollywood-style emotional attachment is imaginary. It doesn't exist. If I intended to wait until I was so over-the-moon in love with a woman that I couldn't live without her, I would simply never marry.

Hmm... That hung me up. It didn't square at all with my previous understandings of romance and how the world works in that regard. I found out later that my pastor was going through a divorce at the time and was perhaps a little jaded. Pastors are often well-trained and highly qualified to advise in these situations. This one was not.

Unfortunately, though, judging myself to be young and foolish and him seasoned and wise, I took his advice. Mistaking my admiration and fondness for my girlfriend to be the closest thing to true love one could ever find, I asked her to marry me.

Dumb.

Key Note

**Seek advice,
but do what's right for you.
Integrity demands it.**

Inevitably perhaps, our marriage soon began to crack. We held it together for longer than we probably should have, but two months before our fourteenth anniversary, our divorce became final.

At about the same time—partly as a result—I began doubting my religious faith. The two great pillars of my life, marriage and faith, were simultaneously crumbling.

How could this be happening?

> *"Who are you?"*
>
> —Pete Townshend

A better question might be: Whose life was I living?

The problem was that it wasn't my own life. I was living a life that had been prescribed for me by others; granted, with my willing participation.

My upbringing had been happy, healthy, safe, complete, and well-suited to a child in the South. The bad news was that I had simply replicated that world on a larger scale without ever considering whether it was how I should live my *own* life as an adult. Consequently I was brute-forcing my way through life like the proverbial bull in a china shop.

It doesn't have to be that way.

Key Note

**Living your own life
increases your likelihood of happiness.**

Clearly, I had work to do. And I set to it with great determination. I studied relationships—my own and those of others. A key truism that emerged is that one *must* establish and get to know oneself. It is critical that we have a firm grasp on our likes and dislikes, what we can and cannot live with, and what we can and cannot live *without.* And that we make peace with those realities. Only then can any individual live an honest life, a life of truth and integrity.

To be clear: While honesty and integrity are excellent virtues in dealing with others, that is not the point here. Being honest with *ourselves,* and true to our *own* needs and passions, will give us our best and happiest lives. And living our own best life will benefit those around us more than living a righteous life that is not our own.

I also studied religion. Realizing that I do not have the ability to speak myself or others into existence, I sought out answers for how we came to be here. In the end, I was successful in finding a religious paradigm and a morality I am comfortable with and that empowers me to deal with realities I do not understand.

Whose Life Are You Living?

How about you? How well do you know yourself? Have you built your life around who *you* really are? Or have you allowed others to define what your life should look like based on *their* understanding of the world?

What is it about your current life situation that nags at you? Where do you feel that something isn't right? Are you actively working to define those hazy notions that won't let you have peace in your world?

Do you understand the issues that challenge your sense of honesty? Are you continuously resolving to do the things that integrity requires? Are you seeking help from trusted advisors who have the ability to help you define the problems and then arrive at workable solutions?

Conductor's Notes

Our best life requires integrity. Which means that we must get to know ourselves. Then comes the hard part: developing the strength to build lives that reflect who we are—not what someone else wants us to be.

It's best to learn these things early, but certainly better late than never!

If your Symphony is to be truly yours, what will you play? If you love jazz, do you feel obligated to play classical music anyway because that's what *real* symphony orchestras do? That would be a mistake. Do you like the rich sound of a full orchestra but want to play in the style of big bands? Play Duke Ellington with your orchestra!

It took some doing, but when the time was right, I met Judi.

Judi's religious views are compatible with my own. She understands my work life because she's a flight attendant for the same airline I pilot for. She's also the single mother of a small child. And the most beautiful woman in the world. And I could no more live without her than I could my right arm.

Judi has helped me understand that Hollywood-style love is indeed real and worth pursuing. We married a few years ago in a beautiful ceremony written by ourselves, presided over by us, and attended by those we love. We have embarked on the difficult and noble journey of joining our lives and those of our children. And we couldn't be more excited and happy together.

Yes, we find ourselves needing to engage in "work" related to our relationship. But we've found that the work our marriage requires has little to do with creating our love. It has to do with finding agreement on peripheral issues, related more to how we spend our time and provide guidance to our children than how we relate to each other on an emotional level.

Judi and I have both completed our walkabouts. We are each comfortable with the person we have become *and* with the organism that is "us." And daily we find redemption in nurturing all three.

"In any moment of decision, the best thing you can do is the right thing, the next best thing is the wrong thing, and the worst thing you can do is nothing."

—Theodore Roosevelt

Chapter 7

If You're Still Breathing, It Wasn't Fatal

YOU'RE IN AN AIRPLANE. Your seatbelt is not fastened. In fact, you're not sitting down. You're at the back of the plane, standing beside the door. And the door is open! The wind noise is so loud you can barely hear yourself think. You're wearing a helmet and an incredibly heavy backpack. And the guy behind you has just slapped the back of your thigh and shouted "Go! Go! Go!"

Do you go?

My First Jump: Career Diversification

SEPTEMBER OF 1991 is when I left the military to join the airline industry. It was a time of great optimism and opportunity. Of course, everyone understood even then that an airline career is somewhat unreliable as a wealth–

generating path, so my excitement at joining the airlines was appropriately tempered. Still, the foreseeable future was bright indeed. So I jumped out of the metaphorical airplane I'd been flying in for many years. Not because I particularly needed to, but because I wanted to.

And things started well in my new career. Even so, to offset the risks of working in the airline industry, I soon started dabbling in real estate and bought a couple of rental houses.

Over the next decade, I invested a great deal of time learning about real estate in anticipation of growing my rentals into a real business. By the summer of 2001, I had five houses in my portfolio. It was a nice start, but I would need more if I were ever to replace my airline income.

Then in September of that year, disaster struck. The devastation of four hijacked airplanes crashing into three national landmarks set into motion a chain of events that would cripple the entire world economy for years.

My airline was one of the two whose jets were taken over and used in the attacks. The emotional effects were beyond description. The economic effects to our company were also immediate and devastating. Within two years, the airline I had cast my lot with was bankrupt.

Jump #2: Investing in Plan B

MY EMPLOYER WALLOWED in bankruptcy for three long, painful years. As that process unfolded, my fellow employees and I learned all about multiple pay cuts and pension cancellations. With my airline income decimated and my retirement plan now less than reliable, I became thankful for my real estate background and the small portfolio I had established before the bankruptcy. It was time to grow my real estate business in earnest.

I understood, like Will Rogers, that "they ain't makin' any more of the stuff," so it should have been a good bet. (This was before we learned about the already-brewing financial and real estate crises that would crush those worlds only a few years later!)

By fall of 2004, I had grown my portfolio to twelve houses and had processed a number of additional real estate transactions. Realizing that I had developed a comfortable working knowledge of contracts, negotiations, and how to evaluate property, I went out and got a real estate license and became an agent. That would be my Plan B should the airline career cease to exist.

Jump #3: Joining a Fixer-Upper Partnership

I WENT TO WORK as a real estate agent in February of 2005. My first real deal didn't close until late that year. But by early 2006, I had found some traction and was working so much that I was able to take a short leave of absence from the airline to work my agency job full time.

Those were heady days. My optimism, all but shattered by the airline's bankruptcy, had returned. I was working long, hard hours, but they were resulting in real dollars in my bank account. I could see myself replacing my lost income by the end of the year, with the potential of replacing my entire airline income within another eighteen months. As of early 2006, my rentals were filled with good tenants and cash was flowing nicely. Good times!

That April, I was approached by another real estate agent with whom I had worked several times over the years. Let's call him Jared. I had found Jared to be trustworthy, competent, and knowledgeable, and we had developed a casual friendship through our previous business transactions. Jared proposed that we buy a property together, fix it up, and then sell it for a profit. He would actively manage the project while I and another investor would provide the financial backing. And he just happened to have the perfect property, as well as a third partner ready, willing, and able to join our project.

Do the numbers!

Because of my previous workings with Jared, I had very few misgivings about the project. The numbers he presented looked good. They had been vetted by an appraiser, as well as the local investment bank, and I was excited about the prospects. So again, I jumped. But this time it wasn't because I particularly wanted to. This time I felt like I needed to.

This would be another step on my way to independence from the airline through my new real estate business.

But I didn't work through the numbers on my own. I was too busy with my other agency work. Besides, I trusted Jared's abilities and judgment.

Trusting Jared's competence in this circumstance was a mistake. Had I done my own due diligence, I would have realized that all of his projections were wildly optimistic. There was simply no way that this project could fly.

The wake-up call was a default notice from the bank in October. By the time we unloaded the property the following January, we had lost our entire investment plus another twenty-five percent.

The very expensive lesson learned: Never trust anyone else with the numbers!

How does that song go again: "What doesn't kill you…"??

MAJOR LOSS. But not fatal.

I am still recovering from that mistake. But recover I will.

Meanwhile, the government had lessons for me as well.

Jump #4: Surprise from the "Infernal" Revenue Service

OKAY, SO MAYBE THIS was more like being pushed out of the plane than jumping of my own volition! Still, I went out that door.

The default notice from the bank arrived in mid-October. On November 6th, I received an audit notice from the IRS concerning my 2003 tax return. Apparently their auditor wished to dispute my status as a "Real Estate Professional" for tax purposes.

A rough several weeks, those.

At the time, the law provided that as long as certain tests were met, real estate investors could deduct all of their real estate expenses against any other income. I had availed myself of those significant deductions, which had been instrumental in helping me survive the pay cuts associated with the airline bankruptcy.

But because I was also a full-time airline pilot, the auditor's assertion was that I did not qualify for Real Estate Professional status, and therefore the deductions for my real estate ventures should be disallowed.

The liability associated with their position was a big number. It amounted to even more than we had lost on the partnership. Yikes!

And so the negotiations began. My advisors argued forcefully that I owed the IRS nothing. The auditor, followed by several other supervisors as we went up the chain, argued that I owed more than I could ever hope to repay! And over the course of two very stressful *years,* I learned more than I ever wanted to know about the machinations of the Internal Revenue Service. How, for example, they use their U.S. Treasury–supported checkbook to try to build court-worthy cases when they smell blood in the water.

Amidst this fight of my life, the 2007 real estate crisis finally hit my rentals. Like anyone else who had invested in single-family homes in the preceding years, I took some major blows to my portfolio. Rents decreased to the point that my rental income was below my mortgage payments. Property values fell until I owed more than the properties were worth. And lending options dried up, making it impossible to refinance. That "perfect storm" meant that for the foreseeable future I would be writing monthly checks to cover business losses out of my household income and life savings. Not-so-good times!

Do I have regrets about plunging wholeheartedly into rental real estate during the airline bankruptcy? Of course. But only in the sense that it didn't work out the way I'd hoped. I absolutely do not regret making the "jumps." It certainly looked like the best thing to do at the time. Sometimes only after the fact do we receive the data that would have changed our decisions. But by then it's too late to avoid the consequences. It's reasonable to accept them, deal with them, and move on.

And then there are times we *have* to jump—or we get pushed out of the plane, as I was during the tax audit. Our own judgment, our own desires in the circumstances, have nothing to do with it. The only question is whether or not we are ready to do what needs to be done once we are out there, freefalling through the air. During those times, we must rely on our preparation to get the parachute open and then strive to regain control and land on our feet.

Ultimately, in all cases, here's what we need to do:

> **Key Note**
>
> **Make the best decisions possible with the information available at the time. And then respond. Make adjustments. Change course if necessary. But carry on.**

Yes, some of my lessons have been painful. Even as I write this, my airline is struggling again and the "B-word" is once more being bandied about in the media. My rental portfolio has suffered during the lending crisis of the last several years; but it still exists, and we are managing. In fact, it looks more and more valuable to my retirement every day that my airline loses money. Those rentals may after all be my golden parachute out of the airline industry.

Speaking of parachutes, you're there at the door of the airplane. The Jumpmaster is slapping your thigh and yelling at you to "Go! Go! Go!" Well?

Do You Jump?

There have been times in the past when we've figuratively jumped out of perfectly good airplanes of our own volition. Maybe in hindsight, it wasn't exactly the right thing to do.

And sometimes we find ourselves at the metaphorical door of the airplane for reasons *not* of our choosing, like an employer gone bankrupt or an IRS wolf at the literal door. Like it or not, something's gotta be done!

So yes. You jump.

But wait a second. Sure, you're standing at the gaping door of a C-141 transport, wearing a helmet and a parachute. And the Jumpmaster is suggesting with some intensity that maybe you oughta step over the side. But it's still a loooooooong way to the ground. How can I say with such certainty that I know you're gonna jump? And how does that Jumpmaster know that you're not gonna stall out his whole line of paratroopers who need to jump before the plane reaches the end of the drop zone?

Most importantly, how do *you* know you're gonna jump?

Seriously. *How do we all know that you will jump out of that perfectly good airplane?*

You can. You just need to *know* you can.

DURING MY TIME at the USAF Academy, I had the opportunity to attend the U.S. Army's Parachute Training Jump School. It was a challenging three-week course. Week one, Ground Week, taught us how to don and check our equipment and to safely execute a parachute landing fall. During week two, Tower Week, we put on our gear and were physically raised on towers high enough to allow us to experience descending underneath an open parachute. Then came week three: Jump Week. This was when we were to apply everything we'd been taught and jump five times out of perfectly good airplanes.

Three different weeks, three different skill sets to master, on our way to earning our "Jump Wings."

It would be an important omission, though, if any description of Jump School did not emphasize that the syllabus consisted more than anything else of physical conditioning. This was in the early eighties—before today's consciousness about maintaining good health. And many of the trainees arrived at Jump School woefully out of shape.

So a large part of the training involved getting us in good enough condition to endure a parachute landing without injury. It was, and I'm sure still is, a rigorous program.

Toward the end of the second week, the instructors had a particularly important lesson in store as we arrived at the training ground early that morning.

Mental strength rules!

WE WERE TOLD THAT we were going on a one-mile run. As we started out, the Jumpmasters set a brisk pace that had us all wondering how in the world we were going to make it to the end of the course without stopping to catch our collective breath.

You've probably seen those television shows or old movies that show a platoon of soldiers marching in formation, singing a rhythmic chant. Chanting helps everyone keep in step, marching together as one unit. And it's done while *running,* too! Singing a chant during physical conditioning helps soldiers keep their breathing rhythmic as well, so they don't get winded so quickly.

On this day at the Jump School training ground, we were singing for all we were worth. And not only to stay in step or to control our breathing. Oh, no…we were using the chants as a distraction from the increasing burn in our legs—and more importantly, as a means of encouraging each other and staying psychologically prepared for (and unified against!) whatever the instructors threw our way.

By halfway through the mile, the Jumpmasters had increased the pace from merely "brisk" all the way to "lung-searing." Hearts pounding, we were feeling the strain in our arms, our legs, and even our bones. We were learning just how hard we could be pushed.

As we approached the finish line, our physical and mental reserves were depleted. To say we were relieved doesn't begin to express the intensity of our emotions!

But the lesson of the day came at us hard and fast as we entered the final hundred yards. The sergeants began telling us that we were not in fact finished. On the contrary, we'd be going for another *full mile* before being allowed to stop!

With that news, the exhaustion became overwhelming. A number of troops dropped out of formation to rest. They *just knew* they couldn't go another mile, so they gave up on the spot.

The blistering reality, though, was that this was a mental test—not a physical one.

Those of us who stayed in formation ran perhaps another hundred yards before we were called to a halt and allowed to rest. As we walked back to join our comrades who'd given up only a few yards short of the end, the instructors said nothing, allowing the lesson to become self-evident: *It's always mind over matter.*

"Mind over matter..." Sounds impressive. But what does it look like? What does "mind over matter" actually mean?

In this particular case, it meant that most of the platoon continued to run. Were we in better physical shape than those who quit? I don't think so. Other dynamics were at work. Several of us were young bucks from service academies, driven to show our mettle. Others were older service members—enlisted and officers—who had waited years to take this training course and were hell-bent not to blow their chance. The one commonality among all of us was this: a simple, undeniable determination not to be defeated.

> **Key Note**
>
> **If you believe you can keep going
> as long as you need to,
> you're probably right.
> If you believe you can't go on,
> you're probably right about that, too.**

Situations like this are classically self-fulfilling. We conclude that we can continue toward our goal, or that we can't. Our thought process here is critical, because we can convince ourselves either way! Which means that our success is up to us. It's all about what we believe. In other words, *it's always mind over matter!*

So there you are in the door, looking over the side. How do you and that Jumpmaster know you'll jump out of that airplane? You both know you're gonna jump because in order to even get to the door, you had to get through Ground Week, Tower Week, and the physical conditioning. You're ready. You both know that you want to, or that you need to, *and that you can.*

So, yes. Absolutely. You go!

What Have You Learned?

We all can see that some jumps we've made have been unfortunate. But we're still running.

How are you managing the long-term ramifications of your decisions from the past? What have you learned from them that will stand you in better stead in the years to come?

Do you regret making those jumps? Or just the way they worked out? How about the way you faced up to the results? Can you release those regrets to the Universe with thanks for the lessons that made you into who you are today?

Conductor's Notes

It doesn't always work out the way we'd like. That doesn't mean we shouldn't go for it when the opportunity comes our way. When you want or need to make a jump, be as careful as you can, learn what can be learned, then *Go!*

Right now you're taking baby steps toward your ultimate goal of standing before your Symphony. At some point the Symphony will become self-sustaining and you'll focus all your energies on that alone. Until then, do what you need to do to keep running and keep the Wheel turning.

Will redemption eventually come to my real estate debacle? Of course. It always does. What about my flying career? Will that, too, eventually heal up? History says it will. I can't see far enough into the future to predict when redemption will arrive or what form it will take. I can, however, see far enough into the past to know that it has come before—time and time again. Because it has already come so many times, I trust that it will again. And until it does, I can, and will, continue to run. I don't know when I'll be able to stop and rest. But I know that at some point, I will. Redemption comes. The Wheel continues to turn.

Something else I know: Someday I'll find myself in a metaphorical airplane yet again, with the opportunity or the necessity to stand up, hook up, shuffle to the door, and then jump. What I hope as I go forward is that between now and then, I'll have prepared myself. I'll have done the Ground Week and Tower Week; I will have done the physical conditioning appropriate to the task. And when a potential "real estate partner" comes knocking, I'll know how to evaluate the situation. Or when I need to do battle with the IRS, I'll understand how to fight that fight. And as those situations unfold, I'll believe that I can keep going as long as I have to. And I'll probably be right.

"Perseverance—a lowly virtue whereby mediocrity achieves an inglorious success."

—Ambrose Bierce

Chapter 8

Prepare. Respond. Keep Running.

MY EXPERIENCE WITH the Colorado Children's Chorale was one of the most significant high points on my Wheel of life. No doubt about it.

Over time, as the memory of that night has settled into my consciousness to be relived again and again, one aspect of it has risen to the surface: A large part of its value to my soul is that one of my own children was part of the chorale that night. Yes, I took joy in the event itself. But my son having been in that choir is like the cherry on the icing on the cake of the day.

In the moment, I couldn't really focus on him. Had I done so, I surely would have caved with emotion. It was good enough to know peripherally that he was with me.

But *now,* I have a visceral contentment in knowing he was part of that experience.

MY ASSOCIATION WITH the Colorado Children's Chorale did not end when my son graduated at the end of that season. As it happened, one of the CCC's artistic staff members had recently resigned. While my participation in my son's concert was in no way a formal audition, my success was enough to get the artistic director thinking.

After the concert, she approached me to discuss whether and how I might fit into the organization on a permanent basis.

Today I serve as a Music Assistant at weekly rehearsals and at concerts throughout the year in venues around Denver. Now when I go to Boettcher Hall, more often than not I'm there to help organize Chorale concerts rather than just sit in the audience. Though I'm not yet the master of my own choir, my affiliation with the CCC has me in many ways living the dream that began so many years ago with my failed audition for drum major.

THE TAX AUDIT is long since over. I was *not* successful in persuading the appeals officer to concede my entire case, though it turned out not nearly as bad as it might have. I paid a pretty good chunk of money to settle with the IRS and an even heftier chunk to my professional advisors for their assistance. As I anticipated, this outcome was painful, but not fatal. I've let it go and moved on to other concerns.

Interesting afterword: Since my case was completed, a case very similar to mine went all the way to trial, and the IRS lost. Talk about redemption! While I won't be able to reopen my own case, the IRS will never again be able to extract taxes not intended by law from real estate professionals in cases similar to my own.

And thankfully, the rental property business is finally recovering. Rents and property values are rising, and banks are more willing to lend. I'm still writing expense checks, but they're smaller than they used to be.

It's now early 2014, nearly seven years after the real estate crisis launched us into the Great Recession. And—mark your calendar—I predict that we have finally weathered this storm. The Wheel of Fortune is turning again! And maybe I, too, have finished my sojourn without a kingdom at the bottom of the Wheel. How is it going to feel to be a prince who is about to reign? What rings are waiting for me even now at the top of this new cycle?

And, you know, I would be remiss if I did not gratefully acknowledge that as dark as these ages seemed at times, every single day during the crisis, my family had food on the table, a roof over our heads, and clothes on our backs.

Key Note

We don't reign at the top of the Wheel indefinitely; nor do we languish at the bottom forever.

HAVEN'T WE BEGUN to realize that the Wheel never *really* stops turning? When one challenge abates, another inevitably rises. We're into the eighth chapter of "stuff" that has happened in my life, but the stories keep coming.

Right after I finally survived that audit was when I broke my neck. Remember *that* from the Preface? And there's more to that story, so hold on. It's about to get bumpy.

The luckiest man alive.

EVERY MAY FOR SEVERAL YEARS, I'd gone to Moab, Utah, with a bunch of friends to do some mountain biking. This particular morning, we drove to the top of the Porcupine Rim trail. At the trailhead, we unloaded our bikes, geared up, and started down the hill.

We had been freewheeling down the slope for about forty-five minutes when I came to a fairly simple challenge in the trail and thought, *I'm going to have to either jump this or go around it.*

That is the last thing I remember from the ride.

As best we can reconstruct the crash, I came out of the saddle at about twenty miles per hour, flew over the handlebars, landed squarely on the top of my head, and tumbled for several yards along the trail before settling unconscious.

I was in a group of ten that day, but since I was tail-end Charlie, none of them was aware of my accident. In fact, no one at all was around to see it happen. But several minutes after I went down, four more riders came along and stopped to help. I learned later that I was so white, they feared they were riding up on a corpse!

As my head cleared and I heard the lead rider call out to me, I took a quick and cautious inventory of my limbs. Recognizing the need to keep my head still, I tried very carefully to move my fingers and toes. I was relieved to discover that three of my four extremities worked just fine. However, I had only limited movement of my right arm, and my right hand was utterly unresponsive.

Hmmm. This could be bad.

Now, I've already mentioned how incredibly lucky I was that my spinal cord remained intact through the crash. But that was only the beginning. *Several* critical things had to go just right in order for me to have a good outcome.

First, the trail I was on meandered all over Grand County, Utah. So I could have fallen far from any vestige of civilization. But where I did fall happened to be just after the trail crossed a paved road. That location also happened

Prepare. Respond. Keep Running.

to have cell coverage, which meant that the riders who found me were able to call 911 right from the crash site.

And because the group happened to have several riders, one was able to go back up to the road to wait for the responders while two more stayed with me and the fourth one dashed down the hill to alert my group that…well…let's just say I wouldn't be rejoining them on my own.

Shortly after that, my good fortune became apparent again. The Grand County Sheriff arrived on the scene before the ambulance and started some basic triage. As any football fan knows, when dealing with a blow to the head, asking the injured person some simple questions helps to determine the potential severity of the injury. The sheriff quizzed me on easy stuff like my name, what day of the week it was, what I'd had for breakfast, etc. When I answered every question without hesitation, we knew that I'd somehow managed to avoid a serious concussion.

Next—the ambulance arrived at the intersection of the trail with the paved road. At that spot, the trail happened to be just wide enough for the ambulance to drive right to me. Had I crashed even a short distance further down the hill, my rescuers would have had to carry me out on a stretcher over some brutal terrain. Instead, they simply lifted me right into the ambulance.

Forty-five minutes later, I was being x-rayed in the Moab Hospital emergency room. This was when we found out just how seriously I was injured. Let's see…over the handlebars, headfirst landing, unresponsive hand…yup, my neck was broken. But I was talking about it!

Here's some more good luck: timing. If this had happened before the age of high-speed Internet, I'm not sure what the protocol would have been; but I'm sure it would not have been this: The ER doc was able to email my x-rays to a neurosurgeon at the regional hospital 113 miles away, who was then able to fire up the flight-for-life helicopter and send it down to Moab for me. Just over an hour later, I was in an MRI tube in Grand Junction.

By then, of course, we knew that my neck was severely broken. But the MRI revealed the details along with the biggest Fortune bundle of all, which was that my hand paralysis was due to nerve bruising outside of the spinal column—*not* a damaged spinal cord.

So let's summarize: a neck broken in five places; several fractured ribs; a hand that wasn't much good at the moment; and road rash on my left shoulder and right leg, which had the hospital staff extracting gravel out of my skin with forceps.

But I was going to live to tell the tale.

Because of how the entire sequence of events *happened to* unfold, my prognosis was as good as it could be. While a complete recovery was by no means certain, it was a possibility.

That was the good news. The bad news was that I was very broken. I spent most of the summer of 2012 lying in bed or in front of the television trying to catch up on *NCIS* reruns through a morphine-induced haze. And in the end, my right hand was going to take some therapy to return to usability.

But so what?

I had survived the crash. The initial crisis was over. At that point, the more important issue became, how was I going to respond to this wreck? Was I going to curse the Universe for spoiling a good weekend on my mountain bike? Was I going to get angry at being confined to my bed for several months? Or was I going to do something else?

> *"Nothing happens to any man that he is not formed by nature to bear."*
>
> —Marcus Aurelius

OBVIOUSLY, THIS STORY is about a pretty significant event in my life. In truth, though, it's also about the life of a very good friend who kept coming to mind during those long days and longer nights when I was hardly able to move.

This friend (who also happens to be named Mark), started his work life as an airline pilot, but in recent years had become an entrepreneur, an author, and a public speaker in addition to flying commercial jets.

So what was it that made me think of him while I was recovering from my crash?

The year before my accident, another accident occurred. Mark's brother and his family were trail-riding in jeeps around Colorado's Front Range. As they exited the trail to head for home, one of the jeeps hit something and rolled. Mark's nephew who is tall, although wearing his seatbelt, was tossed up just enough to hit the top of his head on the roll bar. His neck snapped, his spinal cord was severed, and in an instant he became a quadriplegic at eighteen years of age.

A few months later, Mark was diagnosed with cancer. But they caught it in time and his surgery was successful.

Not long after, he was diagnosed with another form of cancer—this time in his thyroid.

So there he was yet again, standing in the door of an airplane, being pushed out into the wind. What was he gonna do?

Being the kind of guy he is, he was going to do whatever needed to be done. In this case, that meant undergoing more surgery. That surgery, too, was successful; they got the cancer. However, a nerve that controls his vocal cords was nicked and he lost his voice. Suddenly he was a public speaker without the ability to speak.

Finally, in Mark's capacity as a pilot, he worked for one of the major carriers devastated by the events of 9/11.

The list of horrors that emanated from that day is long for all of America, but Mark was particularly close to the tragedy. As it happened, one of the pilots so brutally killed that day was a colleague at Mark's airline. But he was more than just a colleague; he was a mentor and close personal friend. The loss hit Mark hard.

Then, as the world economy descended into chaos, Mark's airline was forced to declare bankruptcy.

Now, corporate bankruptcy may not sound like all that big a deal to someone who's never been through it—happens all the time in the business world, right? But here's what that really looks like: Bankruptcy enables an employer to abrogate every agreement they've ever made with their employees. *Work rules?* Gone. *Benefits?* In the past. *And retirement…?*

Before the bankruptcy, Mark had been looking forward to a comfortable pension in his golden years. But as part of the proceedings, his company simply canceled the pension plans for all employees. Gone. Vaporized. So sorry.

And then they cut Mark's pay in half. Yes, *in half*. No longer able to afford his house payments, Mark lost his home to foreclosure and personal bankruptcy.

Time for another summary. Here's my friend Mark's life over the last few years: friend murdered by terrorists; career disaster; bankruptcy; home foreclosure; quadriplegic family member; cancer times two; surgery complications.

That's a pretty heavy list.

But you'd never know any of this had happened to him unless you knew it had happened to him. He's one of the most positive, inspiring, and fun-to-be-around individuals I've ever known.

How—*how*—can that dichotomy exist in any individual? How can it exist in the world?

I asked him. Here's what he said: "Sometimes life kicks you where it hurts. And you can lie there and moan, or you can get up and move on with what's important."

That was it. He was and still is moving forward. I can't tell you how many times this friend came to mind while I was wearing my cervical collar. And there, through him, was my challenge. Was I going to lie there and moan, or was I going to get up and move on with what's important?

MARK'S VOCAL CORDS eventually healed up and he was able to resume his speaking engagements, inspiring our kids to live life without limits. His nephew has become a motivational speaker in his own right, working in my friend's business. The airline continues to operate.

I recovered from my biking accident and was back in the cockpit only a few months later. I still have some reminders of the incident—my neck is a little stiff and my right hand doesn't work quite the way it used to. And while it's good to have my experience with the IRS over with, like so many Americans, I find myself still dealing with the unpleasantness of the lingering recession. You've read here what that looks like for me.

But you know, I'm still breathing. I'm still running with the Jumpmasters. I'm continuing to kick the Wheel around to the other side or put on the brakes when necessary.

I'm not in complete control of everything that happens. Nor, though, am I completely powerless. I believe I'll ultimately be just fine. And I'm probably right.

Are You Still Running?

How about you? Has the Great Recession or another serious challenge impacted your life? Okay. I understand. But you're still running, right? When was the last time you reminded yourself that you are, above all, still alive? Today, do you have food on the table? Today, do you have a roof over your head? Today, do you have clothes on your back?

Have you reminded yourself that you've somehow managed to get over, under, around, or through all of the challenges in your past—to even get to the point of reading this book right now? Because of that reality, can you imagine that you have the resources to meet the challenges that will inevitably stand against you in the future?

Let's talk some more about how that Wheel never really stops turning. As you continue to live, Fortune is going to present you with an exciting but scary opportunity to do something you've always wanted to do. And she's going to confront you with a dreadful and daunting responsibility. You are one day going to find yourself on the precipice of the airplane looking over the edge at decision time. Something will have to be done. Have you already decided to jump out of that perfectly good airplane whenever you feel that slap on your thigh?

Today, with the Colorado Children's Chorale, I'm absolutely the windshield. With my rental properties I'm the bug. With my airline, who knows?

Five years from now, I'll be five years older. I'll face new challenges between now and then. Great things will happen in my life. I'll revel in them. Bad things will happen as well. I'll deal with them. Five years from now, I'll have more stories to tell. And even more adventures to look forward to.

Five years from now, you, too, will be five years older. What will you do between now and then? How should you prepare for the next time your Wheel turns down? Who are your Jumpmasters who can provide the training and preparation you might need? Where will you go? What will you see? Life will happen between now and then. How will you respond?

Conductor's Notes

The lessons of today are the same as they have been through the ages: Life moves forward (what an exciting thought!); the Wheel of Fortune turns. Sometimes you're the windshield. Sometimes you're the bug. Regardless, the way to success in the end is to keep on running.

And now that we've thought through your present position on your life's Grand Wheel, you have recognized what your Symphony will someday look like. You know who your players will be. You know what kinds of music you'll play. Day by day, you're building. While life is happening around you, slowly but surely your Symphony is coming together.

ONE LAST THOUGHT about all this: When we get busy, distracted by our own Wheels of Fortune, it is critical to remember that ours are not the only lives at stake in how we respond to life.

Our kids are watching.

What will our high school students experience as they grow into young adults? Will our own responses to life's challenges provide good modeling for them? While we proactively equip ourselves to handle the inevitable low points on our Wheels, are we equipping our kids, too, to handle the low points on their own Wheels?

How can we help our teenagers to see their potential and make that potential their reality? Can we demonstrate through our own lives, our own ups and downs, our own highs and lows, that no matter how bad a situation seems, in the words of someone far wiser than me, "This too shall pass"?

If they keep putting one foot in front of the other, if they decide that they can persevere, they'll probably be right. Their Wheel *will* inevitably turn. Their world *will* change. Their redemption *will* come.

"I've failed over and over and over again in my life and that is why I succeed."

—Michael Jordan

Chapter 9
It's Better to Be Right Than Wise

WHEN MY OLDEST SON, Luke, was in middle school, he started pushing pretty hard to play organized football. His mother and I had not encouraged that particular sport because we'd known so many kids who had been hurt. But we didn't want to discourage him either. Kids need to be kids and to experience as much of the world as they can. So as summer gave way to fall the year he turned eleven, we decided to relent.

And join a team he did. I took great pleasure in watching him learn. I had wondered if he'd like it. He'd never been involved with contact sports before, and I really had no idea how he'd respond to the knocking around that is part of the game. I needn't have worried. When he got up laughing after spearing a tackling dummy several times, I knew he'd be fine.

The stars align…

THE TEAM LUKE JOINED was an expansion team, so few of the boys had much in the way of experience. But they were coached by a well-organized staff of enthusiastic dads, each of whom had some level of advanced football experience. It was a fearsome combination: players with no bad habits and coaches who knew what they were doing! They were a joy to watch in early season practices as they came together so effectively.

The first game of the season was one of the greatest days of my life. Luke had earned a spot as a running back, and I can still see him taking a handoff from the three-yard line. He ran to my sideline in an end-around sweep to score the first touchdown of the first game of his first season of football! No father has ever been more proud!

The opportunity appears…

THAT FIRST SCORING DRIVE was an indication of how the entire season was going to work out. The team didn't go undefeated, but by the end of the year, they had earned a berth in the league's Super Bowl.

So there we were, gathered on a frigid November night in a local stadium to watch the boys fight for the championship under the lights. It was a miserable defensive slugfest. After four quarters of heartbreaking battles back and forth across midfield, we came down to the last play of the game. Our team was ahead, 7-4. (Yes, the slugfest had included not one, but *two* safeties!) The other team had the ball at our forty-yard line, so a field goal was out of the question. They had to score a touchdown.

The choice is made…

OUR COACHES PULLED the whole team back off the line to defend against a long throw into the end zone. It was a good strategy. If the ball was thrown, all our players were in place to converge and make sure it got knocked away. If a run was called, they could charge up the field to make the tackle. It looked like the game was in the bag.

The plan is executed…

THE COUNT WAS CALLED, the ball was snapped. It was a pass, deep, just short of the end zone, to the far corner. Our entire team converged on the intended receiver at the one-yard line. A mass of bodies leapt to make the play; scores of hands stretched out to gain control of the ball one last time. We didn't even need to catch it. All we had to do was knock it out of the air!

And then…

THE UNTHINKABLE HAPPENED: The other team's receiver came down with the ball and managed to fall into the end zone for the win.

It's Better to Be Right Than Wise

Our boys were heartbroken. To come so far and get so close, only to have victory snatched away at the absolute last second was more than they could bear. Every one of them wept with disappointment.

Of course, they recovered quickly, as boys do. Especially in light of all that they had accomplished. Despite the loss of the Super Bowl, the season had been victorious by every other measure. And the banquet a few weeks later was a happy occasion. We tied a bow on our time together with joy, and parted ways, eagerly looking forward to the following year.

The process continues...

THE SECOND SEASON, however, was unremarkable. The same staff, the same boys, but a mediocre performance. The team had fun, but they ended up with an even win/loss record and without a berth in the playoffs. It happens. No one was discouraged. But we all resolved to do better when we met again in the fall.

The Wheel comes full circle...

AND SO WE DID! The third year was a replay of the first. Win after win took our boys again to the Super Bowl.

Again, we found ourselves in that same stadium on another cold, cold November night, playing for all the marbles under the lights. Again, it was a defensive slugfest. Improbably, the end approached with a score similar to the one two years before. This time we were ahead by more than a field goal, but still less than a touchdown. Again, the other team had the ball just inside our territory.

How often in life is one given a pristine opportunity for redemption? How often do circumstances that once led to regrets, line up again with exactly the same choices presented?

Who among us cannot think of a time when we've wished for just such a second chance?

Again, the choice is made…

EVERYONE WHO HAD BEEN THERE two years before—boys, parents, and most assuredly the coaches—saw what was happening. As it came time to make the call for the last play of the game in this fairy-tale evening, again the coaches huddled. But this time it was different.

This time I heard the defensive coordinator tell the head coach, "I'm gonna send 'em."

The head coach grinned broadly in answer, and the blitz was on!

There were our boys, standing in the door, the wind roaring by. *Ground Week?* Done. *Tower Week?* Check. *Physical preparation?* Complete. It was time for the coaches to slap them on their thighs and yell "Go! Go! Go!"

Did they go? Oh yeah. With the enthusiasm of players who remember defeat from the past and absolutely refuse to be defeated again.

What happened next will forever be a part of my payoff for undertaking fatherhood. Both teams settled in at the line of scrimmage. The count was called, the ball was snapped. Our boys rushed with all their might. They overwhelmed the offensive line and threw the quarterback for a loss.

The game was over. We were Super Bowl Champions of the thirteen-year-old league!

The stands emptied as we parents poured onto the field to embrace our boys. No tears among the players this time! But you might have seen a tear or two in the parents' eyes. Those of us who had been there two years prior understood the magic of that moment. And our hearts blazed in celebration on that dark autumn night.

Key Note

Wise doesn't always mean right.

TWO YEARS PRIOR, a choice had been placed before the coaches. And using all the wisdom at their disposal, they had made a decision. It was a good decision. A wise decision. But it was wrong.

This night, the same choice—exactly the same—was placed before the coaches once again. They could have made the same decision. It would have been just as wise. Had they pulled the team off the line, all possibilities would have been covered, and the probability of success would have been the greatest.

But their decision *this* time, committing the team to the blitz, left no room for other options. It was all or nothing. It *had* to work.

Years before, the wiser, more conservative choice had led to regret. This night, the coaches took the bolder course, trusting the process to take the boys where they wanted to go. The result?

The boys, in turn, trusted their training and coaching. They stayed in the game. They continued to run. They believed in themselves to the end. They jumped out of that airplane and accomplished one of the great victories of their childhood.

That night they reigned!

What Would You Do Over?

Who doesn't want to be wise when a decision needs to be made? And yet, who hasn't made a "wise" choice, only to realize later that it was the wrong one? It happens. How do you respond?

What have your children's great victories looked like? Were they on the sporting field? The ballet floor? Are they in the crayon-on-construction-paper masterpieces affixed by magnets to your refrigerator? Have you had the joy of hearing your child sing without inhibition in a school or church choir?

Did they face adversities and disappointments along the way? Has your child struggled to learn his numbers and then succeeded? Has she overcome an inability to hold a pencil and then written "I Love You" on a valentine?

Could the ultimate victories have happened had the kids not stayed in the process and returned the next year, or the year after?

What have your own great victories looked like? Have any of them come as second chances? Were they possible because you were still in the game when Fortune offered you a "do-over"?

The Symphony of Your Life / Mark Hardcastle

MICHAEL JORDAN HAS A VISION for his life. It changes as his world changes. In years past, he was an athlete who redefined the game of basketball. Today he's a successful businessman. Why has success come to him? For the same reasons it has come to you and will come to you again: He decided what he wanted to do, learned what he needed to learn, and kept after it until it was his.

There is only one Michael Jordan—and it certainly isn't me. But like Michael Jordan, you and I can be successful in whatever ways we define success. At this stage of life, it's unlikely I'll ever be a Gustavo Dudamel. But I am the conductor of my own Symphony, as I define it today.

Speaking of today…Where are *you* in the process of building your Symphony? What setbacks have you encountered? Are you finding it difficult to recruit your musicians? Your board of advisors? Has the owner of the concert hall changed the conditions for the long-term hall rental?

What have you learned from each difficulty? How will you change your approach next time as a result of these experiences?

Conductor's Notes

Sometimes the "wisest" choice just doesn't work out. If we stay in the game, we have a chance of redeeming the outcome.

Never lose sight of what your Symphony will accomplish. Is it playing today what you want it to play? If so, revel in being on top of the Wheel. If not, make the adjustments required.

Try things. Innovate. Dare to fail along the way. That is the way to ensure the Symphony you have in the end is your own.

LUKE DIDN'T PLAY FOOTBALL in the year following his Super Bowl victory. In fact, he's never played organized football since.

Today's high school teams require a commitment that prevents most kids from participating in more than one sport. My son's passion tended toward baseball, so he decided to go that route. And while he has fond memories of those three years on that football team, he has no regrets about choosing baseball. He's been awarded a four-year college scholarship and has succeeded magnificently.

His mother and I have hopes, but no illusions, about his prospects for continuing baseball beyond college. Either way, we can look back on his days in sports with satisfaction and contentment.

And so can he. My son will no doubt experience difficult times. But the lesson for his young life from that night on the football field was that the Wheel turns. And looking forward, he, too, will know...

Yin follows Yang around their elegant circle of life. Summer gives way to fall, but winter always gives way to spring, which must then become summer again. The sun passes from east to west each and every day; each and every night, it passes from west to east again while we sleep. Sometimes he's the windshield, sometimes he's the bug.

Luke is young, but as he matures into adulthood, he will recognize passions that can sustain him when he's challenged. They will serve him as bright lights in his Dark Ages. When faced with a hard choice, he will seek wisdom, but will temper that with a determination to do the right thing, seemingly wise or not. Then he will act with boldness rarely seen in common hours. And when he makes mistakes, he will stay in the game. Already he knows to press on. Hard times are redeemed. Better times are always ahead. And not just better times. If he prepares, then perseveres, and is ready to jump out of that airplane whenever he wants to or needs to, truly good times will come.

"Success seems to be largely a matter of hanging on after others have let go."

—William Feather

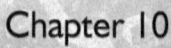

Chapter 10

Creating Your Symphony

IN MY INTRODUCTION, we looked at a number of life-affecting questions. I mentioned that the book's purpose was to spend time with them and generate some thinking that could lead to answers for the issues you are facing right now.

On a larger scale, I've challenged you to think about what you want to do with your life: What would your Symphony look and sound like in an ideal world?

We've also considered how the real world works. Sometimes things go smoothly; sometimes they don't. But "issues" don't have to mean the end of our dreams.

Everything we've thought through has helped us better understand the Wheel of Fortune. But it all remains theoretical until we make it concrete. How do we do that?

How do we go from thinking and understanding to the point of application?

Well, let's see. If "thinking and understanding" is where we begin, and "the point of application" represents where we want to end up, it sounds like we need to take a journey. And a journey needs a map!

I'm a pilot; I like maps. They give us clarity—a beginning, an end, and a navigable route along the way. That doesn't mean we won't encounter bumps, potholes, and detours, especially considering the terrain we need to cover. The question is whether you are willing to deal with such things. Are you determined to find a way over, under, around, or through each obstacle and keep moving forward until you reach your goal?

If you are, let's take these last few pages to review your goals and make them real. Let's draw a map!

Step 1: Define your destination.

YOUR SYMPHONY ORCHESTRA will be the destination on our map. This is the most fun part of the entire process, as well as the most critical. You can't know how close you are to success, or what issues need to be overcome, until you define that success. So let's take some time to enjoy this step. Be as grand and as detailed as you'd like.

Important: You can and should apply the principles we've thought about to any aspect of your life that's "out of tune." Is your vocation out of tune with your avocation? Restore harmony in your work life. Are your family relationships not what you want them to be? Visualize a loving, supportive, and exciting family.

What other personal goals do you have that are not yet realized? Do you want to own your own home? Adopt a child? Visit another part of the world? Use the concepts we've explored to move your Wheel of Fortune in the direction you need it to go.

As author and speaker Mark Hoog suggests in his books and speeches, ask yourself "What if?" What if you could do or be anything in the world? What if nothing could stop you from achieving anything you wanted to achieve? How big would your dreams be in a world like that? Here, now, while you are imagining your greatest life, why not dream *those* dreams? Go ahead! Define your dreams as if nothing could keep you from realizing them.

TIME TO TAKE OUT A PEN AND PAPER, and let's start writing. Brainstorm a handful of ideas that together will define your best work life, family life, recreation life, etc.

Here are some questions that might help get you thinking in the right direction:

- *What does your Orchestra look like?* Put more concretely, what is your ideal career? Living situation? Relationship? Simply, what is your dream? Imagine it fully formed and successful. Make it complete in your mind's eye.

- *What kind of music do you want to create?* When you come to the end of your life, certain memories will

Creating Your Symphony

give you deep satisfaction. What will they be? What might make you wish you'd done things differently? (Don't forget the adage about feeling worse about things left undone than things done badly.) Are you building a life that moves toward the good stuff as much as possible, and avoids those actions that will lead to regret?

- *What instruments will support that kind of music?* What kind of infrastructure do you need to build for what you want to achieve? What people do you need to attract to create the nourishing social circle or career network you imagine for yourself?

- *How many of those instruments will you need?* How much of that infrastructure will you require—and be able to maintain—once your career is in full swing? Will you be the center of a social world with many friends and business contacts? Or will you have just a few key relationships? What do you need to do to create and/or strengthen those relationships?

- *Will you need choral musicians as well?* What kind of partnerships will facilitate your success? Who do you know now who could lead you to your ultimate support network?

- *Where are those players/singers to be found?* How will you attract the partners you'll need? Will you be able to find your support at a local college? Through online networking?

✎ *What is your ultimate venue?* The metropolitan concert hall in the city where you live? Or something more intimate like the local jazz club? Thinking even larger scale, do you want to fill a civic arena? Maybe even a stadium? How about the Red Rocks Amphitheater in Denver? Could you rock the Royal Albert Hall in London? The Acropolis in Athens?

Are you a boutique business person? Will you have a neighborhood storefront? How about a professional corporation? Do you see yourself starting a national chain of franchises? Can you expand internationally?

What does a perfect relationship look like to you? Will your life revolve around a big family? Or just the two of you conquering the world together?

Step 2: Define your starting point.

NOW THAT YOU HAVE a good idea of where you'd like to end up, you need to understand where you are. As a pilot, I learned early in my training that it just isn't possible to navigate successfully to any destination unless you know where you are to start with! Simple, right? But you'd be surprised how many fledgling pilots head off in the wrong direction because they aren't in touch with where they are! In the flying business, we call that "situational awareness." So how is your situational awareness regarding the state of your life? Where are you right now?

A close look at your current life situation will show us the starting point on your map. Which means you need to have an unequivocal handle on exactly where you stand in your world. This part, too, will require some introspection. Today, are you the windshield, or the bug?

Remember that our best life requires truth, so be honest.

- *What is happening today with your Wheel of Fortune?* Is it turning at all, or is it at a standstill? Are you falling away from recent good times? Are you struggling at the bottom of the Wheel with a particularly difficult situation? Or are you rising and about to reign?

- *What is it about your current life situation that nags at you?* Are you actively working to define those hazy notions that won't let you have peace in your world? Are you ruthlessly and continuously resolving to address those notions so you can live with integrity?

- *How well do you know yourself?* Have you built your own life around who you really are? Or have you allowed others to define for you what your life should look like based on their understanding of the world? If so, which prior assumptions do you want to shed?

- *What is it about your chosen career that attracts you?* Is there a subfield you would like to examine more closely? What about where you live? Is it the right city for you? The right housing environment? What do you want your career or living situation to be in five years? Is that your present situation?

- *What is your current level of expertise?* Are you already involved in your chosen field in some capacity, or will you require some training before you can start? Do you know yourself well enough to be the life partner you want to be? Have you been through the school of life to learn what's important to you?

- *How have you arrived at your vision?* Have you shared in successes with people who do what you want to do, or who embody what you want to be?

Step 3: Choose your route.

NOW THAT YOU KNOW where you are and where you want to go, you have to figure out the best way to get there. What do you need to do to get the Wheel turning again in the right direction? How about we start by sending you to Jump School? Go find some Jumpmasters who can make you physically and mentally strong in Ground Week, teach you how to descend under your parachute in Tower Week, and prepare you to jump when Fortune shows you your opportunity. What would Jump School look like for you?

Do you need more education? Would that be a vocational-technical school in your case? Maybe a university degree? How about practical experience? Do you need to join a professional association or trade group so you can internalize what it means to understand, interpret, and then perform in an outstanding fashion? Are there people around you who have experienced life issues that you are facing now?

How about your first steps as a "conductor"? Your first gig probably won't be with the Los Angeles, Chicago, or New York symphony orchestras. Is there a smaller community choir or orchestra that could use your talents while you develop your craft and grow into the stature that your dream orchestra will ultimately require? The sooner you can spend time in your chosen field, the sooner you will begin to hone your skills. Don't be afraid to work as a volunteer if that helps get your foot in the door or on the ladder to success! Depending on what you've chosen as your life's work, it might be wise to start small and grow with time. The most important step is the first one. Start in your field at whatever level you can as soon as you can!

If your circumstances aren't ideal yet, start living as if they are or will be soon. The idea here is to be intentional. Live the way you imagine the person you want to be would live. That may require big changes. But you can make those changes in manageable increments. The musical term is *poco a poco.* Little by little.

Think of proverbs you've heard since you were small: "A journey of a thousand miles begins with a single step." "How do you eat an elephant? One bite at a time." Take those single steps you need to take. And take those single bites one after the other until the elephant is gone!

Do you have appropriate connections? How robust is your artistic network? Could your associations help you find the mentors, experiences, and academic courses you will need to grow to the level you'll want to achieve?

Defining your route will require answers to these and other questions. Be sure to take into account what you've discovered about yourself in the first two steps. Your age and level of determination will be factors as well in what course you set.

If, as I did, you're embarking on a second or third vocation, you may be prepared to take a shorter, more direct route, even if it takes you over steep, rugged terrain with washed-out bridges and other obstacles.

On the other hand, if you are starting your first career and have more time for a less risky path, a more circuitous route with smooth paving and gentle turns through scenic forests and green pastures may be more for you.

Remember…

WHATEVER ROUTE YOU CHOOSE, keep in mind all the realities we've thought through in the preceding chapters:

- In all cases, mental strength rules!
- Your life's patterns will remind you of tools you've used in the past and that you can use again.
- Make the best decisions you can with the information you have. Still, when the gut speaks, listen.

- Learn that you can. If you believe that you can, you're probably right. If you convince yourself that you can't, that will probably become your reality instead.
- Study and prepare so you'll be ready when your chance comes.
- Seek out and embrace those things that will sustain you when the going gets tough.
- Recognize that there will be process failures along the way. We never know how any given situation will work out in the short term. Sometimes it goes our way, sometimes it doesn't. Redefine those results to make yourself stronger and better. It's how you respond that is the critical factor.
- When those "failures" indicate the need for more wisdom, seek out those who have it. But do the numbers yourself before making a decision.
- Respond, adjust, change course, but keep moving. Be determined not to be defeated.
- Some setbacks will not be failures at all, but may occur because some things are out of your hands. You can still learn from them. Remember that it isn't always about you. But that even when it's not all about you, the outcome can be good. Fortune provides allies, sometimes seen, sometimes unseen.
- Be willing to be someone else's ally. Be the spark that changes someone else's life.

- Preparation trumps desire every time. So it bears repeating: *Study. Prepare. Persevere. Critique. Correct. Prepare some more.*

- Fortune provides opportunities. We provide results. We are not merely passengers on the Wheel of Fortune. We have a say in how things go. Don't forget to be on the lookout for your chance so you don't miss it when it appears.

- When you're ready and you see your chance, be bold. *Jump!*

- Finally, if you are to have success in the end, you *must* stay in the process. You will never get to the place you want to be, you cannot win the game, if you stop moving forward while still short of the goal.

And with that, the map is finished. You know where you are and where you want to be. You have some tools to help you get there. And you can count on some bright lights to guide you when it's dark outside. You're ready to begin the journey toward creating the Symphony of Your Life.

It's time to take the first step. Take it! The destination is worth the trip.

Afterword

Where Are They Now?

SINCE THE FIRST PRINTING of this book, I've been approached with the inevitable "Where are they now?" question regarding the other characters in my story. Here's an update:

Randall Stroope, the conductor for whom I substituted at Westside Baptist Church, has gone on to massive success as a composer, having sold millions of copies of his sheet music. I recommend his work without reservation. Check him out at www.zrstroope.com.

The Jumpmasters at Fort Benning have become audience favorites during my keynote speeches. I wish I could personally thank each of them for what they taught me about perseverance and determination. If you are or

Afterword: Where Are They Now?

were an Army Jumpmaster, you have my admiration and eternal gratitude.

After graduation from the American Music and Dramatic Academy, my daughter, Anna, came back from the Big Apple to hone her craft closer to home. Today she's the very picture of a starving artist, keeping body and soul together as a restaurant server by day while remaining active in Denver's musical theater scene by night. I never tire of watching her light up the stage.

My son Luke rounded out his sports career by playing semi-pro baseball for a few summers in Canada. Since hanging up his catcher's mitt for good, he has established a therapy practice in the Denver area for kids who have autism.

My son Seth landed in the Quad Cities, where the Missouri flows into the Mississippi. He's now a restaurateur who creates culinary delights when he's not backpacking around the world. He still sings, but only when he's on a trail.

By the way, you haven't met my fourth son, Cameron, yet. Judi brought him into the family when we married. I expect you'll get to know him in my next volume!

I'm still flying Boeing 777s all over the globe. And I've established a speaking/training/coaching business around *The Symphony of Your Life*. Check out my occasional musings at www.thesymphonyofyourlifeblog.com, and if I can serve your organization with a keynote, workshop, or employee coaching, contact me at mark@symphonyofyourlife.com.

And finally, here in 2017, the Great Recession of 2008 is indeed a distant memory for many. The economy is perking along with unemployment close to pre-recession lows. Real estate prices around the country have recovered nicely and my airline employer is enjoying record profits. It certainly feels like we're at the top of the Wheel.

Which makes the central message of this book all the more important: Challenges are inevitable. The Wheel will turn again. Today is the day to reinforce, rebuild, and gather tools to use when the next series of challenges arrives.

So enjoy your reign at the top of the Wheel. And about that dream that's so big it's going to change the world? Hurry up! We're all waiting on you!

Mark
Summer 2017

Invite Mark Hardcastle

inspirational keynotes

workshops

to Your Business or Event!

executive coaching

www.SymphonyOfYourLife.com

Mark Hardcastle provides coaching to individuals and organizations, helping them face down challenges to achieve greater success in their businesses and lives.

Mark has distilled his own experiences into patterns, which he uses to demonstrate how to get absolute clarity around where you are, where you want to be, and how to get there!

Using humor and stories to engage with his audiences, Mark keeps participants laughing, enabling them to embrace his teachings that have the power to change their lives forever.

Mark's message is for those who want to live *all* of their years—not just live one year many times over!

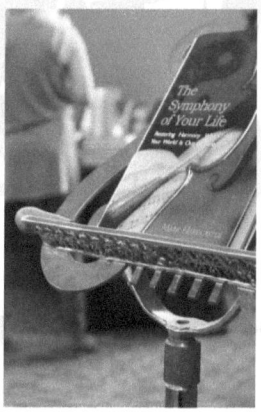

Contact Mark TODAY to start orchestrating *your* best life!

mark@symphonyofyourlife.com
720.840.8361

Mention this page to receive a FREE 25-minute phone consultation!

Connect on Social Media!

 facebook.com/TheSymphonyOfYourLife
 linkedin.com/in/speakermarkhardcastle
 @SOYLMHardcastle

About the Author

MARK HARDCASTLE is a man of many hats. In addition to his successful career as an airline captain, he is a sought-after national speaker, multi-award-winning author, and international consultant and writing coach. He is also a real estate agent and investor, and a music assistant with the Colorado Children's Chorale.

After graduating from the United States Air Force Academy in 1982, Mark served as a pilot for nine years, including combat rotations during the first Persian Gulf War. He left the military in 1991 to join a commercial airline, which he continues to work for today.

When he's not flying big jets over the oceans, you might find Mark at rehearsal with the Children's Chorale, fixing a leaky faucet at one of his rental houses, or outside enjoying the Front Range of the Rocky Mountains with his children. Or, of course, at his laptop writing. This is his first book.

Mark resides in Centennial, Colorado, with his wife, Judi, and son Cameron. His three other children, Luke, Anna, and Seth, are officially off the payroll.

www.ingramcontent.com/pod-product-compliance
Lightning Source LLC
Chambersburg PA
CBHW020649300426
44112CB00007B/308